THE YOUNG CHILD
& Mathematics

Third Edition

Angela Chan Turrou, Nicholas C. Johnson, & Megan L. Franke

National Association for the Education of Young Children
Washington, DC

National Association for the Education of Young Children

1401 H Street NW, Suite 600
Washington, DC 20005
202-232-8777 • 800-424-2460
NAEYC.org

NAEYC Books

**Senior Director, Publishing
& Content Development**
Susan Friedman

Director, Books
Dana Battaglia

Senior Editor
Holly Bohart

Editor
Rossella Procopio

Senior Creative Design Manager
Henrique J. Siblesz

Senior Creative Design Specialist
Gillian Frank

Senior Creative Design Specialist
Charity Coleman

**Publishing Business
Operations Manager**
Francine Markowitz

Through its publications program, the National Association for the Education of Young Children (NAEYC) provides a forum for discussion of major issues and ideas in the early childhood field, with the hope of provoking thought and promoting professional growth. The views expressed or implied in this book are not necessarily those of the Association.

Permissions

NAEYC accepts requests for limited use of our copyrighted material. For permission to reprint, adapt, translate, or otherwise reuse and repurpose content from this publication, review our guidelines at NAEYC.org/resources/permissions.

The "Research Connections" sidebars that appear on pages 16, 24–27, 44–45, 60–61, 66–67, and 74–75 are adapted, with permission, from *DREME TE Project* (Stanford, CA: Stanford University, DREME Network, 2017, 2018), https://prek-math-te.stanford.edu.

The illustrations on pages 31, 32, and 36 are from *There's a Bear on My Chair*, by Ross Collins. Text and illustrations copyright © 2015 by Ross Collins. Reprinted with permission from the publishers, Candlewick Press and Nosy Crow Ltd.

The text excerpt on page 80 and the illustrations on pages 81 and 82 are from *Hush! A Thai Lullaby*, by Minfong Ho, illustrated by Holly Meade. Text copyright © 1996 by Minfong Ho. Illustrations copyright © 1996 by Holly Meade. Reprinted with permission from the publisher, Orchard Books, an imprint of Scholastic Inc., and McIntosh & Otis Inc.

Photo Credits

Copyright © Getty Images: cover (all), 8, 9, 22, 28, 29, 38, 46, 55, 63 (all), 70, 71, and 77

Courtesy of the authors: vi, 2, 7, 10, 19, 20 (all), 30, 34, 40 (all), 42, 45, 52 (all), 57, 58, 59, 61, 64, 67, 75, and 84

Library of Congress Control Number: 2021932769

ISBN: 978-1-938113-93-2

Item: 1157

Contents

Preface

About this Edition

The first and second editions of *The Young Child and Mathematics* (Copley 2000, 2010) have served as resources for teachers of early childhood mathematics that expertly weaved together research-based ideas about development with practical strategies and specific examples. Our goal in this new edition is to extend these strengths to incorporate the latest advances in research and professional development. There already exist numerous wonderful resources about children's mathematical thinking, including *Young Children's Mathematics* (Carpenter et al. 2017), *Learning and Teaching Early Math* (Clements & Sarama 2021), and *Preparing Early Childhood Educators to Teach Math* (Ginsburg, Hyson, & Woods 2014). This book does not seek to replicate those resources; instead, we will bring together the most important ideas about children's mathematical thinking and extend beyond these resources to help teachers not just to *know about* children's thinking but to *use* children's thinking to guide their day-to-day practice.

Over the past decade, we have experienced in preservice and in-service settings the power of leveraging classroom vignettes to support teachers in learning about children's thinking and mathematics content—in ways that are *integrated* and *embedded within* classroom practice. This book contains detailed vignettes from early childhood programs, as if you are stepping into a classroom space where children's excitement is abuzz as their mathematical ideas are being taken up in interactions with other children and with the teacher.

The integrated and embedded approach we take in writing this book will support your learning by engaging with critical aspects of teaching—children's thinking, math content, in-the-moment instructional decision-making—in dynamic and related ways, rather than treating each as separate and isolated. An example of this is our embedded approach to assessment. Because observing children's ideas is at the core of each vignette, we highlight assessment as embedded within teachers' moment-to-moment practice as they watch and interact with children. Connecting instructional decision-making to the development of children's mathematical thinking supports prospective and practicing teachers in understanding the details of what to listen and look for while children are engaged in mathematical activities.

The classroom vignettes and commentary throughout the chapters put children's voices and actions at the center of teaching and learning and showcase responses from teachers that validate and build on children's ideas. This embodies a stance on teaching mathematics that attends to issues of equity and identity: children bring a wealth of knowledge and resources with them into the classroom, and the role of the teacher is to invite children to share these resources as they build on their mathematical understandings. The attention, then, is always on *what children know* instead of what they don't know (NAEYC 2020). This reframing directly challenges prevailing deficit discourses about particular groups of children to recognize and draw from the varied cultural and linguistic resources that children bring to the classroom.

Our Theory of Learning

The writing of this book is guided by a set of important ideas about how people learn—both children and adults. Like many educators and scholars, we see learning as a fundamentally social endeavor. People learn through participating and communicating with one another, in and outside of school. We make meaning through shared engagement in tasks and activities. We learn and communicate through language (spoken and written), gestures, tools, and technology. Who we are shapes how we participate with one another and how we make sense of those interactions. These experiences, in turn, shape how we see ourselves and how others see us.

Research traditions that have influenced schooling in the United States often isolate learning as something to be achieved by individuals. But the individual is only one small tile in the mosaic of learning. Learning does not happen in a vacuum; who you're with matters, the tools and shared understandings of the tools matter, the context matters. People learn as

they share a common experience that leads them to ask questions in a particular way, consider someone else's idea, and maybe build on that idea. We learn as we return to the experience—the same space, the same activity—together on a new day, with new ideas on the table and new ways to engage again.

Not only is learning a social endeavor, it is one that is shaped by broader cultural, political, and historical forces that contribute to ongoing inequality in terms of access and outcomes related to mathematics learning. How children are expected to talk in school is linked to culturally specific discourse patterns. Traditional views of knowing and doing math in school have been narrowly defined, been constrained by Western views of development, and overlooked the varied practices and ways of knowing that children bring with them into the classroom (NAEYC 2019).

This book is driven by a commitment to transform the mathematical experiences of young children. We know that narrow, entrenched notions of what counts as math and who is seen as mathematically capable have led to pervasive and dangerous deficit notions of what children "lack," particularly historically marginalized groups of children. Our hope is that the ideas in this book can provide a vision of learning and teaching that counters these deficit perspectives, recognizes young children's mathematical brilliance,

and capitalizes on their curiosity and intuition. Together, we can create classrooms where children's ideas and contributions are the driving force of the math, where children are active agents of their own learning, and where children see themselves and their ideas reflected in the math we do in school.

Many examples throughout this book focus on the nuance of interpersonal interactions among early childhood educators and children in preschool and kindergarten settings, specifically those connected to the details of children's thinking. Our focus on interactions around children's thinking is grounded in both research evidence and our personal experience. We highlight the critical role of the teacher in crafting meaningful learning experiences for the child. Such experiences leverage the child's individual strengths, unique set of cultural and linguistic resources, history, and ways of participating. Our partnerships with teachers across many settings have confirmed that such a focus is productive (for different teachers at different points in their career trajectories), meaningful (by honoring the varied resources that teachers and children bring to each context), and generative (to support ongoing collaboration and lifelong learning).

The following are the principled ideas that underlie our stance on teaching and learning early math:

> Young children, no matter their age or background, bring with them diverse cultural and linguistic resources and robust mathematical understandings to learning situations.

> The role of early childhood educators is to build on children's intuitive ideas about math, drawing on the resources that children bring as productive learning supports. This can occur in powerful ways across a range of informal and formal spaces in playful, intentional, and developmentally appropriate ways.

> Research documents the development of children's mathematical understandings in early childhood. Attending to the details of children's thinking through the lens of research-based principles supports teachers in recognizing what children understand and making instructional decisions that build from what children know and can do.

> Mathematics identities are socially constructed in ways that privilege and marginalize groups of individuals differently; challenging the status quo of who gets positioned as "good at math" is critical to disrupting inequities.

> Deep mathematical learning occurs through multiple modes of communication—spoken language, gesture, movement, tools, and written representation together play an important role in supporting mathematical development for all children, especially dual language learners.

> Early childhood educators are professionals with vast experience and knowledge about supporting the development of young children. As lifelong learners, they should be supported to try new things, take risks, innovate, and reflect as these processes are critical to long-term learning that is generative.

This set of ideas is not a static collection of words but rather an artifact for engagement designed to exist dynamically as it is read, discussed, taken up, challenged, and adapted by those who see themselves as influential in the lives of children.

Ultimately, our hope is that this book disrupts the narrow ways that individuals have been expected to participate and succeed in mathematics, which have historically produced negative math experiences for children and early childhood educators alike. Our Instructional Activities are intentionally designed learning spaces that reframe mathematical engagement in a manner that is joyful, invite children's participation with a range of mathematical understandings, and support children to make mathematical connections inside and outside the classroom. The vignettes illustrating the Instructional Activities and beyond help teachers reimagine their roles from that of tellers of information to elicitors of children's thinking who nurture the development of positive mathematics identities.

Introduction

Everything a child does has value. A child hops up and down while waiting in line to go outside because they want to know how far they can move their body without getting out of line. A child takes all of the strips of paper the teacher is preparing for a craft and begins lining them up along the edge of the rug because they are curious if there are enough to go all the way around. A child shouts while everyone else is quietly working because they are figuring out how to deal with the frustration of not being able to complete their project as planned.

Early childhood educators already recognize the value in children's actions, observations, questions, and explorations. This book is a resource for a variety of early childhood educators, from those just learning to teach to those with many years of experience, from those who work in classrooms to those in family child care homes—in other words, anyone who sees themselves as playing an influential role in the learning and development of young children. It first and foremost recognizes the amazing qualities of early childhood educators who see the value in everything a child does and who build and maintain safe, nurturing, and developmentally appropriate communities within their learning spaces (NAEYC 2020).

This book capitalizes on that awareness as well as early childhood educators' strengths to see and understand the following idea: Everything a child does not only has value, it has mathematical value.

Let that sink in for a moment. *Everything* a child does has *mathematical* value.

Everything a Child Does Has Mathematical Value

Let's spend some time in two different classrooms to explore what this idea means.

We'll start in Ms. Jackson's classroom, where the teacher is setting up a task to engage the children in some important mathematical work around counting. The children, however, seem to have other ideas about what the task is and how they will participate.

Ms. Jackson pours out some colorful craft sticks in front of a small group of children and asks them to figure out how many sticks they have. All hands pounce on the pile as the children are clearly excited to interact with the craft sticks.

Janae: (*Quietly focuses on taking sticks from the pile one by one, arranging them carefully to create shapes until she eventually builds a square with a triangle on top.*) Look, a house!

Kaylee: ¡Quiero morado! (I want purple!) (*Proceeds to pick out all the purple sticks from the pile.*)

Marco: (*Takes two craft sticks and begins rhythmically tapping them on the table like drumsticks.*) Doo-dee-dee-doo, doo-doo! Doo-dee-dee-doo, doo-doo!

Aito: (*Starts to line up the craft sticks end to end along the edge of the table.*)

What did you see happening? What did you notice? While the children may not have been counting the sticks as Ms. Jackson intended, there was still quite a bit of mathematical work taking place. Let's explore the mathematical value in what each child did.

Maybe Janae's actions caught your eye first. She strategically placed objects in relation to each other, at times orienting them in different directions, and built her craft stick house, composed of two common geometric shapes. In doing so, she was working on important spatial and geometric ideas that you will read more about in Chapter 2. But Janae wasn't the only one engaged in math here. Kaylee, who was excited about the purple craft sticks, was working on identifying important features, or *attributes*, and beginning to sort. As we will see in Chapter 1, children often want to organize collections of objects by attributes such as color, and organizing in these ways supports their counting. Aito, who lined up his craft sticks, might have been doing just this—some organizing before counting. Or maybe he was

Octavio begins to make circular motions with his finger.

beginning to play with some comparisons of length, explored in Chapter 3. Marco, with the "drumsticks," was trying out patterns in rhythms. As we will see in Chapter 4, working to extend things that repeat is central to understanding patterns and algebra.

The children in Ms. Jackson's classroom have hardly just begun and already a great deal of math is happening. One of the goals of this book is to help you notice the mathematical underpinnings of children's participation. But we don't stop there—we also want to explore how teachers might respond to elicit children's mathematical thinking and support the extension of mathematical ideas they are grappling with. We will return to this example later in this chapter with this in mind.

The scenario in Ms. Jackson's classroom happened during a planned math activity, even if what children were doing was somewhat unplanned. There is also much mathematical value happening during the informal spaces of the day, like choice time or transitions; that is, when it isn't "math time." Let's visit Ms. Torres's preschool classroom next and observe an interaction between Ms. Kami, a visiting teacher, and a few of the children as they transition from breakfast cleanup to outdoor time.

> Ms. Kami is chatting with Julian and Victor, who are very excited to go outside and play a game they call "Lava Monster." She isn't quite sure of the full scope of the game, but it definitely involves a lot of running around on the play yard and action sounds! Partway through the conversation, she notices

another child, Octavio, who has been quietly sitting with them at the table. Thinking back, she realizes Octavio has been quiet not only during the conversation about the game but throughout all of breakfast as well. Ms. Kami pays closer attention to him as the conversation continues.

Ms. Kami: When you play Lava Monster, where do you run? Where do you go?

Victor: To run faster, like *ka-zam, zam, zam*!

Julian: Go around in circles!

Victor: Yeah, and then up, then down, like *zoom, zoom*!

Julian: Then down the slide!

Victor: And run away from the Lava Monster!

Julian: I run super-fast!

Octavio: (*Makes circular gestures with his index finger.*)

Ms. Kami: Octavio, so you go around in circles too?

Octavio: (*Shakes his head* no *and puts his hand down.*)

Ms. Kami: Do any of you do anything else when you're running?

Victor: Yeah, we're helpers.

Julian: Yeah, first we take a break, and then . . .

Octavio: (*Starts gesturing other, more winding paths with his finger.*)

Ms. Kami: Oh, are you showing us other ways that you run?

Octavio: (*Quickly nods his head in agreement.*)

Ms. Kami: Wow, check out Octavio's running! How else do you all run?

Julian: I run like Octavio! Around, around, around, then there, and there, and there! (*Makes large, circular motions with his finger followed by zigzag motions.*)

Victor: Like this, really fast! (*Zooms his finger forward and backward quickly on the table.*)

Ms. Kami: Wow, look at all the different ways you run.

A Note About Age

This book is designed to focus on the mathematical learning of young children who are roughly ages 3 through 6, what we consider in the United States to be preschool- and kindergarten-age children. While we care deeply about development and highlight the development of children's mathematical thinking, we are concerned by the fact that, historically, the research foundation for development is culturally specific to White, middle class, Western cultures without being recognized as such (Rogoff 2003). We worry that this sometimes leads to overly universalistic and linear ideas of what math should look and sound like at particular ages, rather than expectations of variation being the norm. We thus refrain from overemphasizing age throughout the book, providing age ranges to add helpful context while not constraining our discussions of development to specific ages.

What did you see happening? What did you notice? This interaction happened during a moment in the day that wasn't "math time," but did you see the mathematical value in what Julian, Victor, and Octavio were doing? These children were deeply engaged in communicating about spatial relations as they described how they wanted to move their bodies, specifically in what directions and along what kinds of paths. As you will see in Chapter 2, describing movement in space is a big idea of geometry and spatial relations. This important mathematical work often happens verbally through descriptive language (*around in circles, down the slide*), as we heard from Julian and Victor. However, it's critical to recognize that children communicate their ideas in other important ways. Octavio, for example, did not say a word during this interaction, yet his nonverbal gestures were essential contributions. He used his index finger and showed what Ms. Kami identified as looking like circles, though Octavio did not really resonate with her questions until his more complicated running paths were acknowledged.

Julian and Victor picked up on Octavio's idea of using gesture to describe running paths; as the conversation continued, gesturing accompanied their verbal descriptions of their movements too.

Interactions like the ones in Ms. Jackson's and Ms. Torres's classrooms might feel very familiar to you. They happen during planned activities and less structured times of the day. They are playful. They are noisy. Children do and say very different things. Some children talk a lot; other children participate by observing and contributing in nonverbal ways (Rogoff 2014). Some are excited to interact with a visitor, while others hesitate. Both of these vignettes demonstrate several important ideas related to child development (e.g., social and emotional learning, gross motor development), but our focus is on uncovering and acknowledging the mathematics that is present. In other words, finding the mathematical value in what a child says and does.

But how do you find the mathematical value when it can take so many shapes and forms? More importantly, how do you leverage and build on it in ways that support children to take the lead? Exploring, reflecting on, and collaborating around these questions is what this book is about.

Finding and Building on the Mathematical Value

Research and policy have drawn the attention of the early childhood field to the critical importance of early math learning, leading educators to consider what all of this means for instruction (Ryan et al. 2020). If everything a child does has mathematical value, should educators just stand back and let the math happen naturally? Observing and noticing, especially through a mathematical lens, are indeed important first steps that give children the space to drive what is happening while also giving teachers the opportunity to take in what children know and are curious about. However, if educators always stood back, children would miss out on some critical learning opportunities. The important work of early childhood educators is to both *find* and *build on* the mathematical value of what children are doing. This is an active teaching endeavor that can look very different across settings.

Consider the vignette with Julian, Victor, and Octavio. Ms. Kami, the visiting teacher, recognized the mathematical value of the circular motions Octavio was using to communicate, and she drew others' attention to his gestures. In doing so, she positioned Octavio's gestures as important contributions to the discussion and found a way to invite Octavio into the conversation while supporting his way of participating, which is quite different from the participation of Julian and Victor. This resulted in Julian and Victor taking up Octavio's use of finger motions as they continued to talk about the running paths, supporting mathematical connections across language, gesture, and movement. Octavio's gestures thus became central to the interaction, opening up an opportunity (with the support of Ms. Kami) to build on and enrich what Julian and Victor had started.

Exploring the different ways that an early childhood educator might respond to children's ideas and actions helps to illustrate the variety of math learning opportunities that an educator could craft in response to children's contributions. The interaction Ms. Kami has with the boys in Ms. Torres's class is just one example; let's return to Ms. Jackson's classroom to analyze another.

Ms. Jackson set up a common math activity found in many preschool and kindergarten classrooms: children are asked to count a set of objects to find out how many are in the collection. However, watching the small group of children interact with the colorful craft sticks, we do not yet see the children counting. How might Ms. Jackson respond to what the children are doing? Below are some possibilities for you to consider in addition to others that you might generate on your own.

To Janae, who built a house with sticks:

> Oh! Can you tell me about your house?

> Wow, how many sticks did you use to build that house?

> Nice house, Janae, but we're counting right now. Can you line up your sticks and count them all very carefully?

> I wonder how many sticks you would need to build another house.

To Kaylee, who picked out the purple sticks:

> You like the purple ones! Now, can you put them back and count all of the colors to find out how many?

> When you finish with the purples, can you find another color?

> Do you think there are more purple sticks or more red sticks? How could you find out?

To Marco, who tapped the table with his sticks:

> You're a great drummer! Can you drum five times? How about twelve times?

> Can you make different drumbeats with those sticks?

> How many sticks are you using to drum?

> After you're done drumming, can you count to find out how many?

> Let's save drumming for another time. Can you tell me when you're ready to start counting?

To Aito, who placed sticks along the edge of the table:

> (*Stand back and observe a bit longer to see what Aito will do.*)

> I wonder how long the table is!

> Can you make sure you're using your own space to count the sticks?

> So how many sticks do you think there will be if you count them?

Think about the range of opportunities opened by each possible response, which will vary depending on the child, their relationship with the teacher, their understanding of counting, the situation, the day, and so on. We also invite you to consider how each response may convey a particular message to the child about their participation and the ideas they are contributing to the interaction. Which responses acknowledge the mathematical value in what the child is doing? Which pursue the intended mathematical goal? How do they follow the child's lead and allow them to drive the math?

An Overview of this Book

Each of the forthcoming chapters focuses on a particular early math domain (counting and operations; spatial relations; measurement and data; and patterns and algebra) to allow for in-depth examinations of children's thinking in that content area. We recognize, however, the relatedness of mathematics learning and understanding and invite you to draw connections across content as you read.

The chapters are built around classroom vignettes that highlight the active teaching endeavor of finding and building on the mathematical value. Discussion of these vignettes is grounded in current research on children's mathematical thinking in specific domains to illustrate the meaningful, while often brief, interactions between teachers and children. Such teaching might take the form of a follow-up question ("Could you count that again nice and loud so I can hear your words?," "Do you think your tower is taller than you?," "Since that didn't seem to work, what else could you try?"), excited and validating words of encouragement ("Wow, you kept turning those pieces around and figured out how to fit them together," "I can see exactly how many dinosaurs you counted

and what they looked like!"), or an offered idea ("Hmm . . . I wonder if the marble will roll forward or backward").

We dive deeply into these vignettes to recreate the experience of stepping into classrooms together. Many are accompanied by occasional "behind the scenes" commentary, sometimes to give you a window into the teacher's thinking and at other times to call your attention to a particular detail within the interaction. The vignettes take place across different parts of the school day, and the classroom spaces during which the vignettes occur are categorized in two main ways:

> **Instructional Activities** are purposely designed to be intentional yet open, supporting children to participate in varied ways as they share and build on their mathematical thinking. The teacher's role within these Instructional Activities is to observe, notice, and respond to assess children's understandings and enrich the mathematics while allowing children's ideas to remain at the center of and drive the activity. One important feature of Instructional Activities is that they are meant to be done over and over. The basic features of the activity remain the same, allowing children and teachers to focus on growing the mathematical work.

> **Informal Spaces** are powerful opportunities to find and build on mathematical value throughout the day, not just during those windows of time where math is the planned primary focus. Vignettes set in informal spaces explore moments in a variety of contexts and interactions—meal and snack times, transitions, indoor and outdoor choice time, storybook reading times, and more—that are rich with math teaching and learning potential.

The classroom vignettes are accompanied by two sections that are critical to the work of an early childhood educator:

> **Exploring Children's Thinking** contains in-depth discussions of the details of mathematical thinking revealed by what children are doing and saying as they engage across a variety of tasks and activities. Knowing the details of children's mathematical thinking supports teachers in recognizing what children understand and making instructional decisions that build from what children know and can do.

A Closer Look at Instructional Activities

Instructional Activities, like the ones we highlight in this book, are not just any activity that a preschool or kindergarten teacher might use in a classroom. (We know that teachers have access to many different activities.) One important distinction of Instructional Activities is that they are meant to be done again and again. The basic components of the Instructional Activity remain the same, giving children a sense of familiarity with the routine of the activity. This allows children and teachers together to focus on growing the mathematical work within the activity and have space for new ideas and innovation.

The Instructional Activities that we share are designed to

- Create a space that supports joyful engagement with important mathematical ideas

- Be driven by children's ideas in a way that showcases the mathematical knowledge and resources that children bring to the classroom

- Help teachers learn about the details of children's mathematical thinking as they engage with children and support children to engage with each other

- Provide enough structure that they are easily learned and implemented but enough flexibility to offer room for teachers to adapt and innovate in response to their own students and teaching contexts

- Encourage children's sensemaking around tools and representation to support mathematical reasoning

- Act as collaborative tools that support teachers to engage with others about their own growing teaching practice

> **Assessing Children's Understanding** illustrates a range of ways that early childhood educators learn about and keep track of children's mathematical understandings across a variety of interactions. We focus here on the in-the-moment assessing that teachers do as children are engaged with each other and the environment. This kind of assessment is ongoing and connected to teachers' everyday practice. While it may occur alongside more formal types of assessment, our focus is how teachers' observation of and learning about children's thinking shapes and informs their decision-making.

Also included in each chapter are the following:

> **Research Connections,** excerpts from resources written by prominent early childhood mathematics researchers from the Development and Research in Early Math Education (DREME) Network that strengthen the connection between research-based information about children's mathematical thinking and what that thinking looks like in practice.

> **Questions from Teachers,** which address inquiries from classroom educators about effectively engaging children in Instructional Activities and other tasks.

We designed the chapters around these common features to support discussions of what children are doing, what you are doing as a teacher, and the details of the math content that emerge—all in the context of classroom practice. By doing so, we highlight the complex and integrated work of early childhood educators in supporting the mathematical learning of children throughout the day (Stipek 2017).

Many of the photos you see in this book come from early learning settings where we authors worked alongside of and learned from educators serving preschoolers and kindergartners across the Los Angeles area, including Culver City, Lawndale, Lennox, Palms, Santa Monica, and West Adams.

To enrich your engagement with this book, the following two appendices are also included:

> **Appendix A** provides a synthesis of current research on children's mathematical thinking.

> **Appendix B** features suggestions for how to support professional engagement and learning while reading this book.

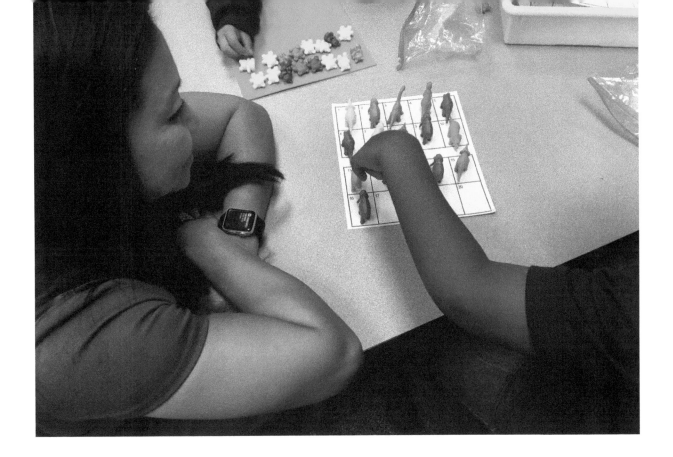

Engaging with this Book

As you continue through this book, you will encounter an assortment of classroom vignettes in which children are engaged with the environment, a variety of materials, one another, and the teacher. These scenarios illustrate what it may look like to find and build on the mathematical value of what children are doing during planned Instructional Activities as well as across more informal spaces. Descriptions of what the teachers do and how they choose to engage with children are not meant to be interpreted as prescriptive or "the right thing to do." Rather, we hope that as you continue to read and explore each vignette, you do so with a reflective lens to consider the opportunities available for children. Moreover, we hope that these vignettes and your reflections can support conversations with other early childhood colleagues to construct together what responsive, developmentally appropriate mathematics looks, sounds, and feels like.

While engaging with this book, we encourage you to make connections to yourself and your own practice and build on your strengths as an early childhood educator. What if, however, you don't see math as a personal strength? If this is the case, you are not alone—the majority of adults don't think of themselves as a "math person" and may experience anxiety around math in general, let alone teaching math. What is important to recognize here is how much our own math identities have been shaped by our schooling experiences and the narrow notions of what counts as math in our society.

Many of us had experiences where being fast with times tables and using the teacher's way of solving problems was what it meant to be "good" at math. While common, this view of math has led only a small portion of the population to think they are good at math and can pursue mathematics-related endeavors. We encourage you to consider mathematics more broadly as creative problem solving, as making strategic decisions while shopping on a budget, as knowing different ways to get to the same location, as working with numbers in your head in ways that are different from what you were taught at school. A broader sense of what counts as "doing math" is important for shaping our own math identities and those of the children we teach.

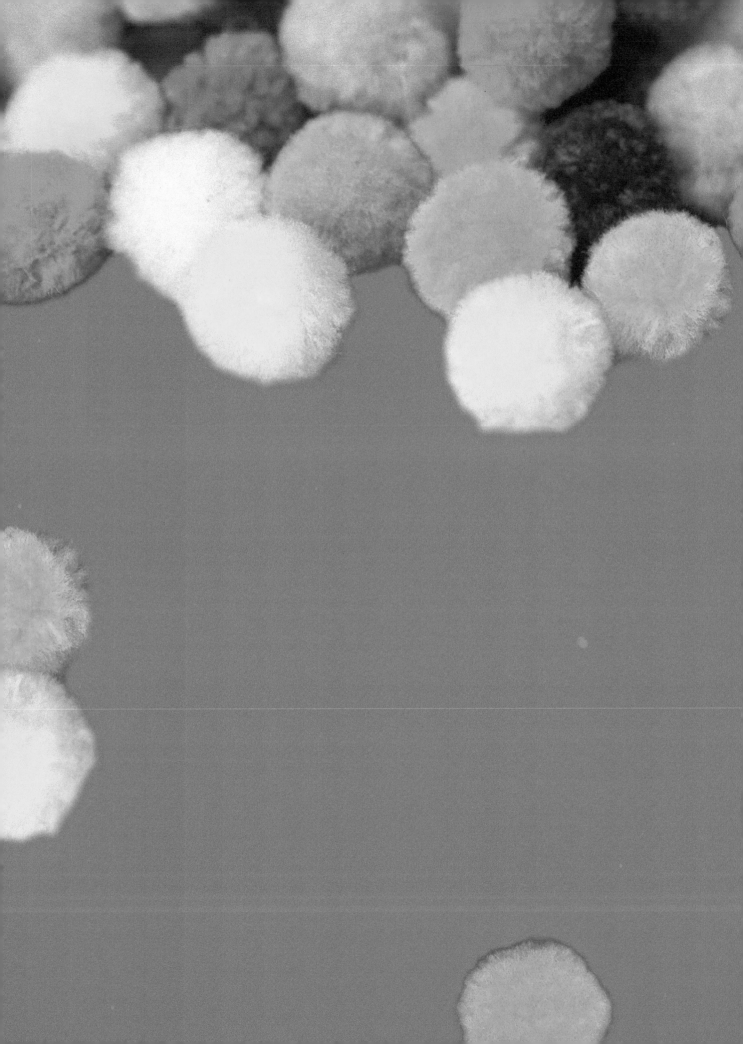

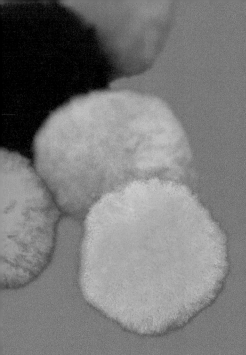

CHAPTER 1

Counting and Operations

Young children count and count and then they count some more! They count things they can see and touch (how many fingers on one hand, how many treats they can have at snack time) as well as things they can't (how old they are, how many minutes until they go outside). While counting may seem straightforward to older children and adults, as young children count to find out how many, they are engaging in complex mathematical work and coordinating many different ideas, such as connecting the numbers they are saying to the objects they are pointing to, touching, or moving as they count.

One idea for early childhood educators to consider is the range and depth of mathematics in counting. There is so much for young children to learn, and having many and different kinds of opportunities to count is essential for young children to continue to develop their mathematical understandings and for teachers to continually take stock of what they are learning about children's understandings. You will see throughout this chapter rich examples of different ways children count, how they are working on coordinating important counting principles, and what this might mean for the child and teacher.

Children use what they learn about counting to begin to add, subtract, multiply, and divide. This is often grounded in real-life experiences inside and outside of school and driven by the need to do things like get more of something, put things together, or pass them out. You will also see examples of how counting can naturally be extended into problem solving with purposeful follow-up questions: *What if you found two more rocks outside and put them in your collection? What if three dinosaurs left the dinosaur party? What if you wanted to share your collection with a friend? With two friends?* What children know about counting and the contexts or stories that can emerge from the collections they count can be leveraged to build understandings of operations, both how they work and the actions they relate to.

The goal in this chapter is to address the teaching and learning of counting and operations as they are worked on in practice, through intentional yet open Instructional Activities and beyond. It opens with a visit to Ms. Gaxiola's preschool classroom and an Instructional Activity called Counting Collections, in which children work on ideas of counting and operations. This is followed by an exploration of informal spaces that support continued learning of counting and operations.

Ms. Gaxiola's preschoolers begin to count collections.

Counting Collections in Ms. Gaxiola's Classroom

Ms. Gaxiola is sitting at one of the kidney-shaped tables, joined by seven of the 3- to 4-year-olds in her classroom: Mattias, Jayden, Aubree, Saavi, Angel, Soraya, and Penelope. Each child has a different collection of objects on the table in front of them—colorful wooden blocks, old keys, bottle caps, counting bears, puff balls, and plastic spoons. There are also some blank sheets of paper and markers strewn about the table.

Mattias is saying one number word for each plastic bear that he stands up. Jayden quickly counts his collection of 21 keys and moves on to make some X shapes with the keys in groups of four. Glancing over at the pile of nine puff balls she has just counted, Aubree reaches for a marker and piece of paper and draws a group of large circles on her paper. Saavi, who has just arrived at the table, is carefully pouring the spoons out of the plastic baggie into a pile in front of

her, making sure her spoons don't interfere with the long line of bears that Mattias has arranged. Angel and Soraya have a large collection of bottle caps in front of them and are working to count them together.

Instructional Activity: Counting Collections

The children are engaged in an activity called Counting Collections. Their job seems straightforward, but it's challenging and mathematically important: to figure out how many objects they have in their collection and make a recording of their collection on a piece of paper. While the objective for each child is the same (to count and find out how many), something that stands out is how each child works on the task a bit differently. This is an important part of Counting Collections—that *each child* is engaged in the task in a way that makes sense to *that child* and that builds on *their* math understanding. This is what differentiation looks like in action! Let's reenter Ms. Gaxiola's classroom to see how the children's participation plays out.

Noticing that Penelope has finished counting and arranging a collection of seven wooden blocks, Ms. Gaxiola asks, "Are you ready to show your collection on paper, Penelope?" She gives her a blank sheet of paper and a marker, and Penelope gets to work. Ms. Gaxiola observes Penelope for a moment before Jayden begins tugging at her shirt. She turns her attention to Jayden and his collection of 21 keys.

Ms. Gaxiola: Yes, Jayden?

Jayden: I'm done counting.

Ms. Gaxiola: (*Looks at his keys, which are arranged in groups of four that resemble X shapes.*) I see that. How many keys do you have?

Jayden: (*Points to one key for each number word he says.*) One, two, three, four, five, six, seven, eight, nine, ten, eleven, twelve, (*Skips thirteen.*) fourteen, (*Skips fifteen.*) sixteen, seventeen, eighteen, nineteen, twenty, twenty-one, twenty-two, twenty-three!

Ms. Gaxiola: So how many do you have?

Jayden: Twenty-three!

Ms. Gaxiola: Wow, you have a lot of keys. Can you count them for me one more time?

Jayden: (*Counts again, using the same sequence and reaching the same final amount.*)

Ms. Gaxiola: Nice counting. It looks like you did something interesting with your keys. Can you tell me about what you did?

Jayden: I made an X with the keys. There's an X, there's an X, there, there, there. But this one is just one. (*Points to the single key that is not arranged in a group of four like the others.*)

Ms. Gaxiola: Ah, you made X's! And how many keys are in each X?

········ Let's follow Ms. Gaxiola for a bit. So far, she has been sitting at the center of the kidney table, watching the children get started on a familiar activity and simply making sure each one has a collection and space at the table.

········ Children are encouraged to move objects and organize them in any way they would like to. While it might look like Jayden is playing with his keys as he puts them in X shapes, the final result is a large collection organized into equal groups. This is foundational work for grouping and place value. Older children might choose to count by fours (*four, eight, twelve,* and so on). Here, even though Jayden is counting one by one, he still gets to experience the mathematical relationships of groups of four within a larger group of 21.

········ Ms. Gaxiola asks Jayden to count one more time so that she can listen closely to his sequence. She is not surprised that, like many other children, he skips some of the teen numbers and is pleased to learn that he can count beyond 20! She files away in her mind for another day to give Jayden a collection with more than 30 objects to see how far he can go in the number sequence.

Jayden: (*Quickly responds just by looking at a group.*) Four!

Ms. Gaxiola: Yes, there are four in that group. Hey Jayden, what would happen if you shared some keys with me? What if you gave me one group of keys? How many would you have left?

Ms. Gaxiola leaves Jayden thinking about the question she has just posed, then turns her attention back to Penelope. Penelope has drawn seven circles on her paper and is in the midst of placing one block on top of each of the circles.

Ms. Gaxiola: How many cubes do you have?

Penelope: (*Uses her index finger to point to each block as she counts.*) One . . . two . . . three . . . four . . . (*As Penelope hesitates, Ms. Gaxiola joins in and points to the blocks with Penelope, counting the last three with her.*) five . . . six . . . seven.

Ms. Gaxiola: How many do you have?

Penelope: Seven.

Ms. Gaxiola: You have seven cubes. You're right. And if I take off your seven cubes, how many circles do you have? (*Carefully slides the blocks off of the paper.*)

Penelope: One, two, three, four, five, six. (*Counts as she points to each circle with her index finger but skips a circle in the middle.*)

Ms. Gaxiola: And this one? (*Points to the skipped circle in the middle.*)

Penelope: One.

Ms. Gaxiola: Yeah, there's one more there. Can you count them over again?

Penelope: (*Starting with a different circle, counts again but skips another circle in the group and still ends up with six.*)

Ms. Gaxiola: Shall we count them one more time?

Penelope: (*Hesitates.*)

Ms. Gaxiola: Maybe you can help me count? (*Points to the first circle at the bottom of the page and waits for Penelope to place her finger on the same one.*) One . . . (*Pauses to let Penelope retake the lead.*)

Penelope: One . . .

An observer might wonder if Jayden remembers that there are four in each group or if Jayden can quickly glance at the arrangement and know it's four. It's unclear in this moment, but this gives us something to look for as Jayden continues to engage mathematically.

Ms. Gaxiola is very intentional about the kinds of support she provides for children as they are counting. She always tries to let the child take the lead because she knows that the moment she takes over too much, she has missed an opportunity to learn about their thinking as they figure it out on their own.

Reflection Question: As you continue reading, what do you notice about when and how Ms. Gaxiola decides to support Penelope's counting?

By removing the blocks from the paper, Ms. Gaxiola is supporting Penelope to make connections between the physical objects that she counted and the written representation that she created. This is important foundational work for children as they develop their representational skills. It is also a rich opportunity for Penelope to coordinate ideas of one-to-one correspondence and cardinality. (See "Principled Ideas in Learning to Count" on page 15.)

Penelope and Ms. Gaxiola: Two . . . three . . . four . . . (*Point and count together. As they reach five, Penelope's counting begins to lose its correspondence with the circles. Ms. Gaxiola slows and exaggerates her count, staying on the fifth circle an extra half second.*) fiiiive . . . six . . . seven!

Ms. Gaxiola: Seven! You have seven here (*Gestures to blocks.*) and seven here (*Gestures to the paper.*). Okay, Penelope, can we put them away and count them into the bag?

Penelope: (*Counts slowly as she reaches for each block and puts it into the storage bag.*) One . . . two . . . three . . . four . . . five . . . six . . . seven!

Ms. Gaxiola: How many did you have?

Penelope: Seven!

Ms. Gaxiola: Seven! You had seven cubes. Thank you, Penelope. Which area do you want to go to next?

As Penelope heads toward the dramatic play area, Ms. Gaxiola watches over her shoulder as Aubree counts her collection of puff balls one last time.

Aubree: Ms. Gaxiola, it's nine! Look, one, two, three, four, five, six, seven, eight, nine! See, it's nine!

Ms. Gaxiola: I see you counted each one and got nine! Hey, I have a question. What if I gave you some more? If I gave you . . . hmm . . . two more puff balls, how many puff balls would you have?

Aubree: (*Pauses, then points at each one and counts in a quiet whisper.*) One, two, three, four, five, six, seven, eight, nine . . . (*Pauses slightly, then points to the empty space next to the puff balls.*) ten . . . eleven! I would have eleven!

Ms. Gaxiola: Wow, you would have eleven! Okay, which area do you choose?

As Aubree heads off to the water table, Ms. Gaxiola notices that Angel and Soraya are sitting quietly with a pile of bottle caps in front of each of them. Ms. Gaxiola decided earlier that she wanted to try something new today: ask Angel and Soraya, who often like to play together, to work together to count a collection. So far, they have each counted their own portions of the bottle cap collection.

Remember that Penelope has drawn seven circles, but the two times that she counts them alone, she gets a total of six. Did she count them exactly the same way, or did she do something different each time she counted?

Ms. Gaxiola doesn't always ask children to count the objects back in the bag, but she recognizes it is another chance for Penelope to continue to work on her one-to-one correspondence. The physical movement of reaching to grab an object and dropping it into the bag can be a support for children to ensure they are counting one number per object.

As Ms. Gaxiola comes up with this question, she realizes that maybe she should have had two more puff balls ready to put out in front of Aubree. She does not have two more on hand, however, and chooses to ask the question anyway. Aubree quite seamlessly completes this new problem-solving task, even without more physical objects to count. Ms. Gaxiola is glad she posed the question anyway, which allows her to see what Aubree is able to do.

Ms. Gaxiola reminds them, "I want you to work together to count these. How could you count all of them?" Angel pushes his pile of caps into Soraya's pile and begins counting quickly as he points to the unorganized pile. Soraya also begins to point and count in an attempt to keep up with Angel.

Giving the partnership some space, Ms. Gaxiola checks back in with Jayden. While she was gone, he took two keys out of his collection and recounted the ones that were left. Then he started stacking the keys to see how high he could make the stacks before they fell. Ms. Gaxiola asks if Jayden wants to go to the block area to continue his building, and he excitedly takes up the offer.

Within a few moments, all of the children have left the kidney table and are off to explore other parts of their preschool classroom.

Having a hard time following all of the children that Ms. Gaxiola is interacting with? Remember that Ms. Gaxiola does this a lot, and this is a familiar way of engaging in math for children in her classroom. Sometimes she quickly checks in with children; other times she spends more time with them one-on-one. What is great about Counting Collections is that you can feel confident that children are engaged in something mathematically productive, with or without interaction with the teacher.

Questions from Teachers About Counting Collections

Counting Collections seems like a fun activity to try out, but is it really something that teachers do over and over again—even once a week or more?

The structure of Counting Collections might seem somewhat simple, but there is so much room to adapt the activity to support children's continued development over time. Teachers love engaging children in this activity throughout the school year and well beyond the preschool and kindergarten years (Franke, Kazemi, & Turrou 2018). Here are some ways that this activity might vary and grow:

- **Build your "library" of counting collections.** It is often easiest to start with materials that you already have in your classroom (e.g., counters and math manipulatives), but soon you and the children you teach will start to see collections everywhere, in school and at home (e.g., paper clips, bottle caps, leaves, socks). This is a great opportunity to connect with families and children's everyday lives around counting.

- **Change up the quantities in the collections.** Go "big" one day to give children an extra challenge in organizing and working further on their counting sequence. Go "small" another day to give extra attention to representing the collection. Encourage children to try something different from what they've done before.

- **Support collaboration.** Ask children to work together to count their collection. Encourage them to talk through a plan with their partner about how they want to count. Help support the different ways that partners might try to work together.

- **Offer different tools and support materials.** Some children prefer to organize their collection in an egg carton or on a grid. Others might look to different classroom resources to find the numeral they are trying to write. Providing colorful crayons gives children the opportunity to represent items using color, an option that would not be possible with a pencil or a single-color marker.

The Young Child and Mathematics, Third Edition

Observing how Ms. Gaxiola engages children during Counting Collections gives a peek into one of the many ways teachers might use this playful yet intentional activity and shows why this activity might become a regular part of a classroom. Teachers and children love engaging in Counting Collections over and over again as there is much room for variation and growth.

Counting Collections not only supports important learning for children, it provides many opportunities for teachers to learn about children's mathematical thinking. Understanding how the details of what children say and do relate to their developing understandings of counting and operations allows you to recognize what children know and respond in ways that support their ongoing sensemaking.

Exploring Children's Thinking: Counting

As young children count things in and outside of school, they are figuring out how counting works and what it tells you. (See the list of principled ideas that children must make meaning of while learning how to count on this page.) If you look back through the interactions in Ms. Gaxiola's classroom, which counting principles do you see children using? What are they still working on? And in what ways does their teacher respond to build on what she learns about their counting?

You might have noticed that as Jayden counts his keys, he skips 13 and 15 but otherwise uses the standard number sequence. Ms. Gaxiola knows that not only is this common for young children but that Jayden's sequence displays an emerging understanding of how the names of the teen numbers are built. The teen numbers that begin with number names (or number words) from the one through nine sequence (*four*teen, *six*teen, *seven*teen, *eigh*teen, *nine*teen) are used in order, while others (*thir*teen, *fif*teen) are skipped. Ms. Gaxiola also notices that when Jayden counts his keys a second time, he uses the same sequence (the stable-order principle).

Principled Ideas in Learning to Count

The Sequence of Number Words. Counting involves using a consistent, ordered sequence of number names (the stable-order principle). Extending the number sequence involves making sense of the patterns of the base-ten number system.

One-to-One Correspondence. Exactly one number from the counting sequence is assigned to each object in the collection (the one-to-one principle).

Cardinality. The last number assigned to an object in counting a collection represents the total quantity of the collection (the cardinal principle).

Finally, Ms. Gaxiola recognizes that when asked how many keys are in his collection following his count, Jayden responds by saying "twenty-three," consistent with the last number he said when counting (the cardinal principle).

Ms. Gaxiola's work with Penelope, in contrast, focuses on supporting the development of one-to-one correspondence. When counting, one-to-one correspondence is about matching each and every object with a number name and counting each object once and only once. Note that a child can accurately use the one-to-one principle without using the standard counting sequence. For example, if a child counts a collection of eight toy cars by touching each car exactly once using the sequence "One, two, free, four, five, eight, nine, eleventeen," they have assigned a single number name to each object (and thus accurately applied the one-to-one principle), even though they have used a nonstandard sequence in doing so. One-to-one correspondence also requires keeping track of what has been counted and what still needs to be counted. Children sometimes do this by moving each object from one (uncounted) pile to

To watch videos featuring Ms. Gaxiola and her class engaging in Counting Collections, scan this code or visit http://prek-math-te.stanford.edu/counting/classroom-videos-counting.

another (counted) pile. Children might also choose to place objects into a line before counting; in some cases, this can make it more challenging to maintain correspondences for a number of reasons (e.g., objects too close together, gesturing too slow or too fast, knocking the objects over accidentally). Ms. Gaxiola's invitation to have Penelope count her blocks back into their bag supports Penelope in working on one-to-one correspondence by connecting each number word that she says with the action of picking up and putting a single block into the bag.

Knowing how children's understandings of counting develop allows you to support different aspects of counting as children continue to engage in Counting Collections. Jayden is working on extending his understanding of the number sequence. Penelope is working on one-to-one correspondence. It is important to recognize that as children grapple with making sense of these interrelated ideas, the understandings that surface will vary depending on the child, the situation, and the moment. For example, one child might demonstrate consistent use of one-to-one correspondence while using a nonstandard counting sequence. Another child might struggle to keep track of which objects have been counted and which have not but show that they can extend the counting sequence into the 20s or 30s and respond to "how many" by stating the last number they used in counting. The same child might count one way with one set of objects on one day, and then differently the next day.

Recent research demonstrates that as children are learning to count, their use of the counting principles does not necessarily follow a single developmental sequence (Johnson et al. 2019). An implication of this finding is that children do not need to know the standard number sequence before counting objects. Rather, Counting Collections can be the beginning of developing understandings of the number sequence, one-to-one correspondence, and cardinality in relation to one another. The openness of the activity means that teachers can invite children to count collections even as their ideas are still emerging; you can focus on different mathematics for different children, depending on what you observe about the child's thinking. There are many productive ways to participate in the activity, and each child can participate and build from what they know in a way that works for them.

To watch videos related to the development of counting skills, scan this code or visit http://prek-math-te.stanford.edu/counting/additional-counting-videos.

Research Connections

The Structure of Number Words

by Herbert P. Ginsburg

With experience counting, children learn to pick up the underlying structure of number: ten is the basic unit (e.g., twenty, thirty) and we tack units onto the tens (e.g., twenty-one, twenty-two). The rules for saying the English number (or counting) words from eleven to nineteen are especially hard to learn because they are poorly designed. *Eleven* should be *ten-one*, just like twenty-one. *Fifteen* should be *ten-five*, like twenty-five. Continuing, each of the tens words resembles a unit word: *forty* is like *four*, *eighty* like *eight*, and so on.

Fifty comes before *sixty*. (A fairly minor problem is that *twenty* should sound more like *two* and ideally should be *two-ten*, *thirty* should be *three-ten*, and so on.) After saying a tens word, the child appends the unit words, one through nine. Learning to count 20 and beyond is children's first experience with base-ten ideas.

For more about young children's early number learning, visit the DREME TE Project's website at https://prek-math-te.stanford.edu.

Adapted, with permission, from H.P. Ginsburg, "What Children Know and Need to Learn About Counting," *DREME TE Project* (Stanford, CA: Stanford University, DREME Network, 2017).

Exploring Children's Thinking: Operations

Operations is a major focus of mathematical learning for school far beyond early childhood. Children will spend many years adding, subtracting, multiplying, and dividing different kinds of numbers and, hopefully, understanding important mathematical relationships across the operations and numbers. This mathematical work happens in preschool and kindergarten as well, but of course not in the same ways it does in later years. Counting Collections can provide an entry point into making sense of the operations.

When Ms. Gaxiola asks Aubree how many puff balls she would have if given two more, she is using the collection as a context to engage in problem solving. To solve this problem, Aubree does not need formal understandings of addition or the plus sign (+). Rather, she uses what she already knows about counting and getting more of something to figure it out, counting her collection again and then counting the two more (imaginary) puff balls that Ms. Gaxiola has given her to find that there would be 11! Eventually children will come to see that to solve problems like these, they do not need to recount the entire collection; instead, they can just count on two more from nine. Given time and opportunities like these to solve problems in ways that make sense to them, children will naturally begin to use more mathematically sophisticated strategies (Carpenter et al. 2014).

In another moment, Ms. Gaxiola asks Jayden, who is counting the keys arranged in groups of four, to consider what would happen if he gave one group of keys to her. How many keys would he have left? Here, Ms. Gaxiola poses to Jayden a take-away or separate problem situation, or what adults might identify as subtraction. In doing so, she specifically draws upon Jayden's choice to organize his collection into equal groups of four. In the vignette, we left Jayden pondering this question to watch Ms. Gaxiola work with Penelope. Had we followed Jayden, we would have seen him push one group of keys far away from his collection and then recount the 17 keys he had left with his same counting sequence, which would lead him to a total of 19.

It is important to note that Ms. Gaxiola decides to pose a problem to Jayden even after he counts his collection "incorrectly." After hearing Jayden count the keys twice with a nonstandard sequence, you might have been surprised that Ms. Gaxiola did not choose to follow up by asking him to count again or to count with her as she vocally led the sequence through the teens. Instead, she gives him an opportunity to solve this problem scenario, knowing that in doing so, he would be engaging in something mathematically powerful while having yet another opportunity to continue working on his counting. Ms. Gaxiola recognizes that it can often be worthwhile to invite children to engage with a challenging math task (a take away or separate problem-solving situation), even if they are still working on what might be considered an earlier skill (counting). Opportunities like these allow Jayden to continue to work on counting *through* solving problems. This example highlights how mathematical work is connected, *not* a sequence of isolated skills that should be worked on in a linear manner.

Connecting activities like Counting Collections to problem solving provides opportunities for children to build on what they know and develop rich understandings in foundational mathematical work. So far, we have discussed *getting more* puff balls and *giving away* keys—these are representations of addition and subtraction posed as follow-ups to counting situations. Teachers might not think about inviting young children to engage with multiplication or division, but preschoolers and kindergartners are often quite capable of making sense of and solving these more challenging problems (Carpenter et al. 2017). They can readily engage with real-life situations that involve grouping and sharing objects, like how many mittens four children will need, how many crackers to put on each plate so that everyone gets the same amount, and how many cups to grab if each cup can hold five cotton balls. You will see an example at the end of this chapter in which a child has an opportunity to share pretend lollipops equally with a friend.

Assessing Children's Understanding

Attending to the details of how children count and solve problems allows early childhood educators to integrate assessment into their ongoing practice. It also allows teachers to focus assessment on what children know, as opposed to what they do not yet know. By setting up intentional yet open tasks (such as Counting Collections) and observing how children use counting throughout their day, teachers can learn much about children's understandings of counting and problem solving. This chapter has provided several different ways that children count and solve problems. You might consider reviewing the vignette in Ms. Gaxiola's classroom through the lens of this question: *What might I want to keep track of related to assessing children's counting and problem solving?*

We captured a page out of Ms. Gaxiola's notebook where she chose to jot down some notes related to the children's understandings of counting and operations. Like any teacher engaged in formative assessment in real time while managing all of the needs of her class, this list is not exhaustive, nor would we expect it to be. It captures meaningful details of children's mathematical work and reveals Ms. Gaxiola's reflective thinking about next steps to find out more and build on children's understandings. Compare what you noticed while reading the vignette earlier in this chapter to what Ms. Gaxiola documented.

Ms. Gaxiola's Counting Assessment Notes

Child's Name	Details of Their Thinking	Wonderings and Next Steps
Jayden	○ Counting sequence into the 20s (skipping only 13 and 15) ○ Counting sequence has a pattern ○ Uses 1:1 and cardinal ○ Makes equal groups of 4 ○ Takes away a group and recounts	Give a larger collection to see if he knows sequence above 30
Penelope	○ Counts to 7 ○ Working on 1:1 ○ Working on cardinal ○ Does well counting objects into a bag	Maybe try a collection that can be stood up (bears?) to see if helps her w/ 1:1
Soraya and Angel	○ Working on counting together!	
Mattias	○ Uses 1:1 well	Maybe partner with Penelope?
Aubree	○ Can represent collection using circles on paper ○ Can join 2 to her collection	

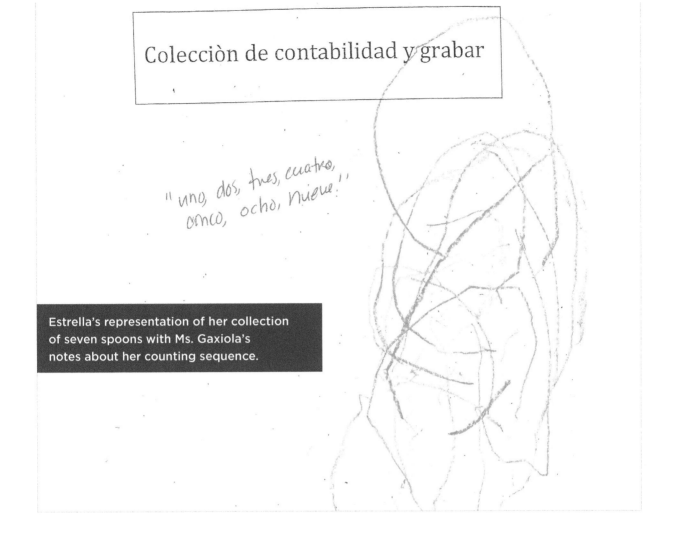

> Coleccìon de contabilidad y grabar
>
> " uno, dos, tres, cuatro, cinco, ocho, nueve."

Estrella's representation of her collection of seven spoons with Ms. Gaxiola's notes about her counting sequence.

On some days, Ms. Gaxiola also takes brief notes on the children's written representations of their collections. For example, early in the school year, Estrella counted a collection of seven plastic spoons from the local frozen yogurt shop. When asked to show her collection on paper, Estrella drew several overlapping loops and curved lines (see above). After asking Estrella about what she created and listening to her count her collection again, Ms. Gaxiola took a moment to write out the number word sequence Estrella used: "*Uno, dos, tres, cuatro, cinco, ocho, nueve*" (One, two, three, four, five, eight, nine). This allowed for Ms. Gaxiola to have a record of Estrella's counting sequence directly on her written representation, which might be useful as a comparison to future opportunities to capture Estrella's counting (say, while counting another collection, washing her hands, or walking up the steps to the second floor). She might also use this work to inform state assessments about Estrella's growth in the number sequence, have a conversation with Estrella's grandmother about her learning, or share with a colleague at a staff meeting as a learning experience that excited her today.

Each day in interactions across settings, formal and informal, Ms. Gaxiola gains detailed knowledge about what the children know and can do. For instance, she sees that on some days and in some contexts, a child shows that they can use one-to-one correspondence throughout their count, while in other contexts, such as when counting a collection that cannot be moved, that same child counts objects twice. The accumulation of this information helps her to create a more comprehensive portrait of the nuances of the children's mathematical understandings. This also helps her know what opportunities might support the children to extend their mathematical ideas as well as make sense of the more formal assessments she has given.

On page 20, there are more representations young children created after counting collections of objects. What do their representations reveal about their understandings? What kinds of questions would you ask to learn more about their ideas? Are there particular notes you would jot down about their counting and/or their representations?

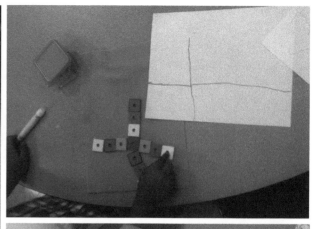

Additional representations made by children during Counting Collections.

In the top-left photo, you might notice the color correspondence between the counting bears and the crayon-drawn circles. (Look carefully, the yellow is hard to see!) After studying the top-right photo, perhaps you would point to one of the white squares and ask where that object is in the drawn representation. You could ask Graciela, featured in the bottom-left photo, to tell you more about the numeral 6 next to the purple square, keeping in mind that this is the first time she is using numerals to represent a group. You may observe in the bottom-right photo that Maya has successfully represented her idea of "a lot," but that the quantities of orange squares and plastic gemstones don't match.

The next set of examples extend beyond Ms. Gaxiola's classroom. As you read through them, consider how a teacher like Ms. Gaxiola might continue to learn about children's mathematical thinking across a variety of contexts and interactions.

Counting and Operations in Informal Spaces

Like all meaningful mathematical work, powerful engagement with counting and operations also happens outside of structured learning opportunities like the ones explored so far in this chapter. Learning about and supporting children's understandings of counting and operations can take place in the informal spaces that exist throughout the day. Let's visit some classrooms to see what mathematical work can look like in those informal classroom spaces.

In each scenario, you will see children using mathematics to explore and talk about their world. Watching and listening for how children engage in counting and solving problems in the informal aspects of the classroom enables teachers to learn more about what children know and can do and creates openings to leverage those understandings in situations they create, either in the moment or later. These opportunities abound in preschool and kindergarten, and while productive on their own, they can also be leveraged by teachers to support mathematical sensemaking and explaining.

As you read through these interactions, consider the following:

> What are the children doing?

> What is the teacher's role?

> What math opportunities are available in this space?

> Are the math opportunities the same or different than in other spaces?

> How are the children driving the mathematical work?

At Breakfast

Ahtziri is still working on her "push-pull" skills to open the package of apple slices that came with her breakfast, so she asks Mr. Nuñez to help her with it. Mr. Nuñez notices Ahtziri's excitement that there are four apple slices in her package. (Did Ahtziri subitize? Count it silently? Mr. Nuñez isn't sure!) As she happily chomps down on one apple slice, Mr. Nuñez takes up the opportunity to say, "Wow, you had four apple slices, and then you ate one! How many apple slices do you have now?" Ahtziri points at the remaining apple slices through the clear packaging and counts, "One, two, three. There's three!"

While Washing Hands

After spending time outdoors, the children line up to wash their hands. It is a routine to wash for 20 seconds and count while washing. Benjamin lathers up with foamy soap and counts, "One, two, three, four . . ." Ms. Bailey notices that he gets quiet after 12 and begins to count with him (". . . thirteen, fourteen, fifteen, six—") before he loudly picks back up again and continues by himself all the way to 20.

While Transitioning to the Rug

Children slowly trickle to the rug as they finish washing their hands and get ready for the activity coming up. Emanual and Kendi take advantage of this transitional time to tell Ms. Navarro about their time outdoors on the monkey bars.

Emanual: They're too hard to me!

Ms. Navarro: Did you swing like this? (*Gestures with her arms from one bar to another.*)

Emanual: No!

Kendi: He just did this. (*Reaches and grabs for an imaginary bar.*)

Emanual: I got three!

Ms. Navarro: Oh, you swung three times?

Emanual: But I didn't got another one. (*Puts an exasperated hand to his head.*)

Ms. Navarro: (*Makes slow, reaching gestures.*) So you did one . . . two . . . three . . .

Emanual: I missed the one!

Ms. Navarro: Oh, you wanted to get one more?

Emanual: I fall down.

Ms. Navarro: So, Emanual, so you went three times—one . . . two . . . three . . . (*With reaching gestures.*)—but then, if you would've gone one more time, how many times would you have gone?

Emanual: Um . . . one time.

Ms. Navarro: I know you missed one time. So you did (*With reaching gestures.*) one . . . two . . . three . . . and then it was going to be. . . ? (*Holds her hand out for a fourth reach.*)

Emanual: Four!

During Outside Time

The children in Ms. Ahadian's class convert the outside playhouse into a McDonald's drive-through. They ride vehicles around the yard and make a stop at the drive-through window to order. The children inside make a sign with a menu using pictures: Hamburger: 2, Drink: 1, and French Fries: 1. One child rides up and orders "a lot" of fries. The child at the window gives her two plates and says, "That will be two dollars." There is no exchange of money and the child rides off as the next child approaches the window to order.

To watch videos featuring more operations work in informal spaces, scan this code or visit http://prek-math-te.stanford.edu/operations/classroom-videos-operations.

During Dramatic Play

Some children are playing "piñata" and collecting pretend candy from the floor. Mr. Hurtado sees Willa counting the eight lollipops she picked up and asks, "So how many more lollipops would you need to have ten?"

Later, Willa decides to share her lollipops so that she and Charlie will have the same amount. Willa puts the lollipops between herself and Charlie and deals out one lollipop at a time, back and forth, until there are no more left to be shared and both children have four.

•••••• Mr. Hurtado poses to Willa a "change unknown" problem scenario in which Willa has to figure out how many more lollipops she would need in addition to the eight she already has in order to reach the desired amount of 10. What do you think Willa might do to figure this out?

Some of the examples you just read might feel similar to the work you already do in your classrooms, such as supporting children to count verbally to 20 or highlighting when there is one more or one goes away. Others you might not have considered, such as posing a "change unknown" problem scenario as Mr. Hurtado does. What other situations come to mind that could offer opportunities for work on counting and operations, and how might you deepen children's mathematical sensemaking in those spaces?

Conclusion

Counting and operations hold great importance in early childhood, providing the foundation for so much future mathematical work. While you likely already knew this, perhaps the nuance and complexity of all that children know, do, and understand as they engage in counting and operations explored in this chapter has led you to think more deeply about supporting children's understandings of such a foundational content area. We see that young children can engage in counting and solving problems in productive and evolving ways, some that you might not have expected, and that we can use what we know about children's thinking to inform what happens next. What details of children's understandings about counting and operations are you intrigued to discover more about?

Making Sense of Operations from a Child's Perspective

by Megan L. Franke and Angela Chan Turrou

When we come across a word problem, we often jump directly to thinking about what operation the problem is asking for. Is it an addition, subtraction, multiplication, or division problem? Once we have decided which operation the word problem is asking for, we then decide what strategy we want to use to execute that operation. Though this approach to solving mathematics problems might be common for adults, it is quite far from how young children approach problems. Young children approach word problems not by thinking about an operation, but by thinking about the story. They consider what objects are in the story (Is it about frogs or bananas or children on the playground?) and what is happening to the objects in the story (Are they hopping away or being eaten or running around together?).

Let's dig into this idea of a child's perspective and how it might differ from an adult's perspective by taking a look at three word problems:

1. Liz had 6 apple slices. She ate 4 of them. How many apple slices does Liz have now?

2. Liz has 4 rocks in her collection. How many more rocks does Liz need to collect so that she will have 6 rocks?

3. Liz has 6 snow globes and her brother has 4. How many more snow globes does Liz have than her brother?

An adult might look at these word problems and see a common operation (subtraction) across all of them. They might think about subtraction as take away and use the strategy of "six take away four" to solve all three problems and get the common answer of two.

A young child, however, would not see a common "six take away four" situation for all three problems. Liz might think about a take away, removal, or separating action for the apple slices problem because if she eats some of her apple slices, then these apple slices would need to be taken away, removed, or separated from the whole quantity. However, a young child would not act upon the other two problems in the same way. The rocks problem has a joining action, as Liz needs to figure out how many more she should join to her current quantity. The snow globes problem is a comparison situation that involves two distinct quantities (six objects and four objects) and asks how these quantities compare to each other. Technically, nothing is happening to these objects; they are just sitting there, nothing joined, nothing separated.

The chart on page 25 is organized to help you see important distinctions among addition, subtraction, multiplication, and division in word problems. Problems that are most applicable to young children are included in the chart. What do you notice about the chart and how it's organized? How would a young child solve each problem? What number sentence could you write that matches the problem situation? (Note: This last question is a "trick question" for the compare problem.)

Examining these three problems the way a young child would allows us to see why a problem might be difficult and what strategies the child is likely to use. How might a young child solve the rock collecting or the snow globes problem? Would they solve both of those the same way? In the next section, we discuss how young children intuitively approach word problems by modeling out the action or number relationships involved.

Beginning Strategies for Problem Solving

Young children solve problems intuitively. They know that when crackers are eaten, they take away. They know that when a child has LEGO bricks and is then given more, the LEGO bricks join together. When they hear a story problem, they naturally try to act out the problem using counters. Attending to what happens in the story enables children

Selected Word Problems for Addition, Subtraction, Multiplication, and Division

Action/Relation	Examples	
Join *(add to)*	*(Result Unknown)* Rogelio had 3 toy cars. Her grandmother gives her 2 more toy cars. How many toy cars does Rogelio have now?	*(Change Unknown)* Rogelio has 3 toy cars. How many more toy cars does Rogelio have to find to have 5 altogether?
Separate *(take from)*	*(Result Unknown)* Rogelio had 5 toy cars. She gives 2 toy cars to Kadyn. How many toy cars does Rogelio have now?	*(Change Unknown)* Rogelio had 5 toy cars. She gives some to Kadyn. Rogelio now has 3 toy cars. How many toy cars does Kadyn have?
Part-Part-Whole *(put together/take apart)*	*(Whole Unknown)* Rogelio has 3 blue toy cars and 2 green toy cars. How many toy cars does Rogelio have altogether?	*(Part Unknown)* Rogelio has 5 toy cars. Three are blue and the rest are green. How many green toy cars does Rogelio have?
Compare	Rogelio has 5 toy cars. Kadyn has 3 toy cars. How many more toy cars does Rogelio have than Kadyn?	

Equal Group Problems	Example
Multiplication	*(Product Unknown)* Dylan had 3 plates. He put 4 Goldfish crackers on each plate. How many Goldfish crackers altogether did he put on the plates?
Measurement Division	*(Number of Groups Unknown)* Dylan had 12 Goldfish crackers. He put the Goldfish crackers on plates. If he put 4 Goldfish crackers on each plate, how many plates did he need?
Partitive Division	*(Group Size Unknown)* Dylan had 12 Goldfish crackers. He put the Goldfish crackers on 3 plates with the same number of Goldfish crackers on each plate. How many Goldfish crackers did he put on each plate?

Adapted from and informed by Carpenter et al. (2017) and NGA & CCSSO (2010)

to figure out what the problem is about and what to do to solve it. The more explicit the action (and the more the children understand the context of the story), the easier it is to solve. When story problems build on actions and situations children know and materials are provided, children can often readily solve simple addition, subtraction, multiplication, and division problems.

The strategies children use to solve story problems are robust and used across many different types of problems. Knowing the set of possible strategies they may use can help you know what to listen for as they solve problems and support instructional decision-making. We are going to focus on the two types of strategies that are most common for young children: direct modeling and counting strategies.

Direct Modeling

Alma and her teacher are sitting on the carpet together, and the teacher poses three story problems. Alma has counters in front of her. The teacher reads the problems aloud to her as many times as she needs. Alma solves each problem by doing what the problem describes; she uses her counters to map out the action without any prompting from the teacher.

Problem 1: Alma had 3 LEGO bricks. Her dad gave her 4 more LEGO bricks. How many LEGO bricks does she have in all?

Alma counts out three counters and puts them in a pile. She then counts out four counters and puts them in their own pile. She pushes her two piles together and counts them all, saying, "One, two, three, four, five, six, seven."

Problem 2: Alma had 6 LEGO bricks. She gave 2 LEGO bricks to her brother. How many LEGO bricks does Alma have left?

Alma counts out six counters and puts them in a pile. She takes two out of her pile and moves them across the floor, away from her original pile. She counts the counters that are left saying, "One, two, three, four. Four left. I have four left."

Problem 3: We have 3 boxes. If there are 2 LEGO bricks in each box, how many LEGO bricks do we have in our boxes in all?

Alma gets up and finds three pieces of paper. She tells the teacher that those are her boxes. She puts two counters on each paper. She then points to each counter and counts, "One, two, three, four, five, six."

In each of these situations, Alma solved the problem in a way that matched the problem situation itself. She followed what the problems said and counted out the sets. In the first problem, she made her set of three, then her set of four, and then showed that she knew the action in the problem was joining by pushing the sets together and counting them all. Since she made the set of three and the set of four and counted them all together, we would say she directly modeled the action in the problem.

Alma used direct modeling for each of the three problems. In the second problem, she made the set of six, took away the set of two, and counted those remaining—another count-all strategy. In the third problem (a multiplication problem), she created the groups by using pieces of paper, put two LEGO bricks on each, and counted them all.

Direct modeling is a robust strategy that children often use instinctively to successfully solve problems that we might not even consider giving at a young age (such as the multiplication problem Alma solved, or even multistep problems that involve cookies in boxes and eating some of them). Experience solving problems by directly modeling the action paves the way for more sophisticated strategies to emerge.

Counting Strategies

Now let's look at where Alma would go next in her solving of these same three problems. Once she has had experience solving problems like these by direct modeling, she will eventually stop making her initial set and use a counting strategy.

Problem 1: Alma had 3 LEGO bricks. Her dad gave her 4 more LEGO bricks. How many LEGO bricks does she have in all?

Alma starts with three (in her mind), then grabs four counters. As she touches each one she says, "Four, five, six, seven. I have seven LEGO bricks." She could also keep track on her fingers instead of using counters. Here she would count, "Four, five, six, seven," putting up one finger each time until she had four fingers up, signaling that she is finished counting.

Problem 2: Alma had 6 LEGO bricks. She gave 2 LEGO bricks to her brother. How many LEGO bricks does Alma have left?

Alma starts with six (in her mind), puts up two fingers, and counts back "Five, four," putting a finger down each time. She says, "Four LEGO bricks left."

Problem 3: We have 3 boxes. If there are 2 LEGO bricks in each box, how many LEGO bricks do we have in our boxes in all?

Alma puts up two fingers for the LEGO bricks in each box. She counts them three times: "One, two," then "Three, four," then "Five, six; six LEGO bricks."

Again, there is a pattern to Alma's counting strategies. In each case, she did not need to make all of the sets and represent every LEGO brick in the story. In the first two problems, she did not make the initial set of three or six LEGO bricks, and in the last case, she did not make the three boxes. She abstracted those and only made the second set. This strategy builds from the direct modeling strategy; it still follows the action in the problem and requires doing what the problem says to do, but it does not require making all of the sets. This is a more advanced strategy than direct modeling, and it is more likely to emerge in a problem like the first (3 + 4), especially if the number being added is small (getting two more, for example).

As you watch children solve word problems, you will see them use all kinds of materials to support their solutions. It is important to look beyond what materials they use and instead look at how they use the materials. As we saw with Alma when she was solving six LEGO bricks take away two LEGO bricks, she could use her fingers or she could put out counters; in both cases, she would make six and take away two. Both of these are direct modeling strategies. Looking at how the child uses the materials enables teachers to differentiate direct modeling and counting strategies. Being able to differentiate these strategies helps you see that children are making progress in their understanding of the operations and will enable you to consider which problems to pose next and what materials might be helpful for children.

For more about young children's operations learning, visit the DREME TE Project's website at https://prek-math-te.stanford.edu.

To watch videos featuring more examples of problem solving, scan this code or visit http://prek-math-te.stanford.edu/operations/additional-operations-videos.

Adapted, with permission, from A.C. Turrou & M. Franke, "Making Sense of Problem Types," and M. Franke, "Beginning Strategies for Problem Solving," *DREME TE Project* (Stanford, CA: Stanford University, DREME Network, 2017).

CHAPTER 2
Spatial Relations

The previous chapter took a deep dive into how children interact with numbers throughout the day, including how they count and operate on numbers to make them bigger or smaller or share them. Numbers are often (and understandably) the main focus of early math conversations, so the importance of the ideas discussed in the previous chapter may not necessarily feel new. This chapter shifts away from numbers to another important early math content area: spatial relations.

Traditionally, spatial relations and geometry are talked about together, and shapes often get the spotlight within this content area (e.g., learning the names of different shapes, integrating shapes into arts and crafts activities, finding shapes in the world around us). However, this is just the tip of the iceberg. While identifying shapes and beginning to learn their attributes is a component of this work, there is so much more to the work of geometry.

People often think of geometry as the mathematics of shape, but it is also the mathematics of *space*.

So much of young children's learning is about developing a sense of themselves in relation to the world around them. Consider this quote from German mathematician Hans Freudenthal (1973):

> Geometry is grasping space . . . that space in which the child lives, breathes, and moves. The space that the child must learn to know, explore, conquer, in order to live, breathe, and move better in it. (403)

What is powerful here is that geometry is not just the set of rules and definitions and vocabulary words that often come with geometry lessons. Geometry, rather, is about *the child* interacting with the world in which they live; as they do this, they explore position, direction, and movement through space.

Viewing geometry in terms of grasping space—or spatial relations—helps us think about the range of experiences children have throughout the day. Children experience geometry as they move their bodies throughout the classroom; build, stack, and piece together LEGO bricks to make a castle; figure out how to arrange their drawings and the letters of their name on paper; tell a friend where to find a book; arrange themselves into a line for outside time; and count and move objects from one pile into a new pile to keep track of what they have counted. While movement, gesture, and language are important throughout learning, pay close attention to their highlighted importance throughout this chapter as children engage with geometry and spatial relations.

In the previous chapter, you read about Counting Collections, an Instructional Activity that teachers like to use regularly in their classrooms to support learning of numbers and operations, as well as written representation, collaboration, and other important ideas. This chapter explores another Instructional Activity, called Describe-Draw-Describe, that teachers use regularly to promote spatial reasoning. We follow early learning coach Mrs. Jordan as she engages children in Describe-Draw-Describe in both a kindergarten and a preschool classroom. Following these vignettes is a discussion of spatial relations throughout a variety of informal spaces.

Instructional Activity: Describe-Draw-Describe

Describe-Draw-Describe starts with an image, often a page from a children's book. The title of the activity tells the rest—children describe what they see, draw what they see, and then describe what they have drawn. It might not look like a math activity on the surface, but by focusing on how the teacher engages with and follows up on children's ideas, in-depth mathematical work around spatial reasoning will reveal itself. A major part of the activity is the describing, which doesn't just involve a small set of math vocabulary words related to position. Instead, it happens with a lot of different words, gestures, and movements that children might hear and use in their everyday lives. Listening to and seeing how children communicate their ideas while building on those ideas in ways that simultaneously engage both the individual child and the whole group is another important aspect of this activity.

Describing and Drawing During Story Time with Mrs. Jordan

Mrs. Jordan is greeted by excited children who are eager for her visit. As an early learning coach, she regularly spends time in classrooms across her site. As she gathers the kindergarten class into a semicircle around her, she holds up the cover of a new book, *There's a Bear on My Chair,* by Ross Collins, that she is excited to introduce during story time. This is a rhyming story about a frustrated mouse who wants to sit in his chair but can't because there's a bear on it. The children giggle as Mrs. Jordan introduces them to the cover of the book and begins reading.

Mrs. Jordan: ". . . We do not make a happy pair, a mouse and bear with just one chair." Tell me about what you see.

Utisah: The mouse is mad!

Mrs. Jordan: He's mad. How do you know he's mad?

Children: He's pushing! He's pushing the bear! He wants the bear off!

Mrs. Jordan: He's pushing. Which way is he pushing? Can you show me pushing?

Children: (*Excitedly demonstrate pushing action with their hands.*)

Jasmine: He's pushing his feet!

Elizabeth: But the bear is too big!

• • • • • • • • While Describe-Draw-Describe can be implemented using a variety of images, Mrs. Jordan chooses to integrate it with story reading. She has chosen a fun children's book with a fairly short story and illustrations that she is going to use to spark the children's interest and ideas.

• • • • • • • • Mrs. Jordan picks up on the children's excitement and takes this opportunity to connect what they are seeing and describing to movement in space. She continues to engage the children in movement throughout this opening as she invites everyone to explore Utisah's idea.

He is so **big,**
it's hard to share.
There isn't any
room to spare.

We do not
make a happy pair,
a mouse and bear
with just one chair.

The mouse is pushing the bear.

From *There's a Bear on My Chair,* by Ross Collins. Text and illustrations copyright © 2015 by Ross Collins. Reprinted with permission from the publishers, Candlewick Press and Nosy Crow Ltd.

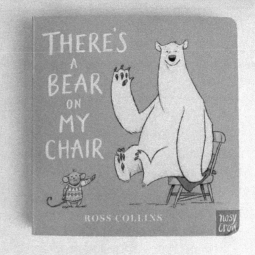

From *There's a Bear on My Chair,* by Ross Collins. Text and illustrations copyright © 2015 by Ross Collins. Reprinted with permission from the publishers, Candlewick Press and Nosy Crow Ltd.

Mrs. Jordan: Oh, the bear is big. Do you think the mouse can push the bear off the chair?

Children: No!

Mrs. Jordan: Why not?

Children: The mouse is too little. He's so little!

Utisah: But maybe he's super strong—like a superhero!

Mrs. Jordan: Oh, maybe he's super strong! If the mouse pushed the bear off the chair, which way would the bear go?

Nicolas: He'd go that way. (*Makes a quick downward motion with his hand.*)

Mrs. Jordan: He would go which way, Nicolas? Which way are you showing us?

Nicolas: Like this! (*Holds his forearm upright, then makes a falling down motion with his arm and slaps the ground.*)

Mrs. Jordan: Oh, like this? (*Holds her forearm upright.*) Can you put your arm up like Nicolas?

Children: (*Also hold their arms up.*)

Mrs. Jordan: Then how does it go? (*Joins in with the children as Nicolas repeats the movement.*) Hmm, I wonder if the bear would go forward or backward.

Mrs. Jordan loves reading this story and experiencing children's reactions. Children giggle at the sight of the bear combing his Elvis-style hairdo. They groan with the mouse's ever-growing frustration. They laugh loudly as the mouse jumps out in his bright green underwear. Making sure not to interrupt the rhythm of this suspenseful story too much, Mrs. Jordan continues to find moments to engage children around what they are seeing and noticing. They excitedly point out the dotted line going from the mouse's "nasty glare" to the bear's eyes.

•••••••• Mrs. Jordan makes an intentional teacher move here by offering more formal mathematical language (*forward, backward*) to provide the children with an opportunity to connect their understandings to this language. She does not hold the expectation, however, that children's use of these specific terms is the only way they can show their understandings of these ideas.

They are intrigued by the mouse's tail and observe how curled or straight it is, especially on the pages where the mouse is clearly moving.

In the preschool classroom next door, before beginning to read, Mrs. Jordan spends time asking the children to describe the cover of the book.

Mrs. Jordan: See that bear? What is the bear sitting on?

Children: A chair!

Mrs. Jordan: A chair! But there's something else . . .

Felipe: Mouse!

Mrs. Jordan: There *is* a mouse. Do you notice anything else about the chair the bear is sitting on?

Koa: There's a pillow.

Mrs. Jordan: Ah, so wait a minute. I heard Koa say that there's a bear on a chair, but there's something else. There's a pillow. Koa, can you tell me where that pillow is?

Koa: (*Sitting at the back of the rug, points toward the book.*)

Mrs. Jordan: I see where you're pointing. Now, Koa, can you use your words to tell me where that pillow is?

Koa: It's on the chair.

Mrs. Jordan: It is on the chair. Where on the chair is it, exactly? Is it above or below the polar bear?

Koa: Below!

Mrs. Jordan: It's *below* the polar bear. Does someone have a different way they would say that?

Shivani: It's under the polar bear!

Mrs. Jordan: It's *under* the polar bear. Who has another way to say it?

Aanik: On the bottom?

Mrs. Jordan: It's *on the bottom* of the polar bear. Or it's under the bear. Or it's below the bear. Is the pillow below the chair?

Koa: No.

Mrs. Jordan: Where is it on the chair?

Koa: On top of the chair.

Mrs. Jordan: The pillow is *on top* of the chair. So the pillow is in between that big polar bear and the chair. He's squishing that pillow flat.

Koa: So flat! (*Holds his hands out and pushes his palms together.*)

It is common for children to respond just as Koa does—by pointing, or by pointing and saying "Right there!" In these moments, there is an opportunity for the teacher to encourage the child to build on this use of gesture with verbal description. See how Mrs. Jordan validates Koa's use of gesture, then follows up by asking him to describe where the pillow is using words.

Note that Mrs. Jordan isn't necessarily expecting specific vocabulary; rather, she is attempting to get a range of ideas on the table. The children can use any language, informal or formal, to say more; each contribution is important. One way that Mrs. Jordan conveys that each child's idea is important is by asking for more than one way to describe the location of the pillow, even though Koa gives a perfectly suitable response. Additionally, this gives children multiple ways to think about the same idea, supporting a deeper understanding of the mathematical relationship.

Exploring Children's Thinking: Describing Spatial Relations

As Mrs. Jordan engages the children throughout this storybook reading, she picks up on children's interests and ideas and skillfully uses a variety of follow-up moves to highlight and build on those ideas. As you can imagine, Mrs. Jordan could have taken up many opportunities to build on a variety of mathematical ideas in other content domains (e.g., measurement, counting, patterns), but she chooses to focus on supporting children's developing understanding of spatial relations.

One mathematical idea that Mrs. Jordan makes efforts to highlight is describing the position or location of an object. There are many examples of this throughout the vignette; you heard the children describe the position or location of the pillow (*on the bottom, on top of the chair, under the bear,* and *below*). As you saw, this specific descriptive language doesn't always happen right away. It might start with children pointing (and saying "Right there!"), but the teacher building on these responses encourages children to use more descriptive language over time. Additionally, focusing specifically on the pillow

creates an opportunity for the children to consider a more complex relationship: since the pillow is simultaneously on top of the chair *and* underneath the bear, the children are pushed to explore and coordinate the spatial relationships among all three of these objects.

The children in the preschool class Mrs. Jordan visits use a variety of words to describe the same spatial relationship. This is important to consider as you support children's development of spatial reasoning because it directly influences how you might engage children. In many classrooms, a teacher might ask children a question, and when the teacher gets the response they hoped for (the "right" answer), they move on from the interaction to the next question or idea. When Mrs. Jordan engages the children, however, she asks more than one child to talk about the same idea ("Who has another way to say it?"), even when a productive answer has already been voiced. Note that she does not ask children for a different idea altogether at this moment; instead, she asks for *the same idea to be articulated another way*. This conveys a number of important ideas about participating in a mathematical discussion, including that there is more than one way to talk about an idea, it's not just about using the math vocabulary, and you should keep thinking and offering your ideas, even if they are different. These ideas are important because they invite a lot of children to participate in a lot of different ways. They also give access to multiple ways of reasoning and articulating an idea, which supports deep conceptual understanding (Moschkovich 2012; NRC 2001).

So far, we have focused only on the verbal communication seen in the vignette, but there is also a great deal of nonverbal communication Mrs. Jordan supports that is important for mathematical learning. Gesture, gaze, and movement play important roles in children offering their ideas as well as engaging with the ideas of others. Koa points to communicate where the pillow is. Children are engaged in the pushing movement and arm gesture to describe how the bear might fall off the chair. These movements are enhanced as Mrs. Jordan follows up on children's contributions by asking other children to join in, such as when she invites the rest of the class to do Nicolas's arm movement. She sees the interaction as a quick and fun way to leverage some mathematical richness, both engaging the children in each other's ideas and incorporating body movement into the mathematical discussion.

Describing Spatial Relations

As children engage in talking about (describing) their ideas about spatial relations, make note of how they

- Name objects ("Flower, flower, bird," "I see a mango!")

- Name and describe the details of objects ("His tail is wavy," "The road is bumpy," "His swimsuit is orange and has dots")

- Describe objects in relation to other objects ("The mouse is wearing a sweater," "She's kicking the ball")

- Describe objects in relation to spatial cues ("The mango has leaves on top of it," "Its tail is going up at the end," "The chicken is inside the house")

- Identify elements of shapes ("It has pointy corners," "This side is long and straight, but that one is short," "That one is tippy; it's going to fall over")

- See shapes within shapes and make shapes from other shapes ("The house has a square on bottom and triangle up there," "There's a big rectangle and a little rectangle and a circle and it's a door," "Triangle, triangle—that makes a square")

- Describe objects in relation to orientation ("The newspaper is upside down," "The boat is turned over," "He's sitting sideways")

- Describe and predict movement ("It will go way down," "He will fall on his back")

- Use mathematical language ("If you turn, um, ro . . . rotate the page like this, the box will be right-side up," "That looks like a square with another straight line going that way")

While some ideas may build on each other, other discussions might encourage different ideas to surface.

To watch videos related to the development of spatial reasoning through Describe-Draw-Describe, scan this code or visit http://prek-math-te.stanford.edu/spatial-relations/classroom-videos-spatial-relations.

Describing and Drawing During Story Time with Mrs. Jordan (continued)

After the children spend time describing what they see, Mrs. Jordan transitions into the next part of the activity: asking the children to draw what they see.

Mrs. Jordan: Okay, I want you to keep in mind all of those great ideas about what you saw on this page. Now you get to go draw what you see on this page. Remember, when we do this, do you have to worry about drawing it perfectly?

Children: No.

Mrs. Jordan: Right! It's about drawing what *you* see. And your drawing might be different from the drawing of the person next to you.

• • • • • • • • Note how Mrs. Jordan works hard to emphasize that it is about each child drawing what they see.

The children head to their tables, where there is paper and pencils for them to use. Children begin to draw as they look up at the page displayed at the front of the room. They draw a little, look up, draw a little more, then look up again. Mrs. Jordan and her teacher's aide walk around the room and talk to the children as they are drawing.

Reflection Question: If you were to try this in your own classroom, how would you make sure that children understand the open-endedness of the task and that it is about expressing their ideas through drawing (not about reproducing the illustration)?

I'll try to tempt him with a pear,
to **lure** him from my favorite chair.

But he just goes on
sitting there.
Why won't he
go back
to his lair?

FREE PEAR!

The mouse tries to lure the bear with a pear.

From *There's a Bear on My Chair,* by Ross Collins. Text and illustrations copyright © 2015 by Ross Collins. Reprinted with permission from the publishers, Candlewick Press and Nosy Crow Ltd.

The Young Child and Mathematics, Third Edition

Mrs. Jordan: (*Pulls up a chair to sit at a table next to Addie.*) Can you tell me about your drawing?

Addie: I'm drawing a polar bear.

Mrs. Jordan: I see that. Where did you start?

Addie: I started right there. (*Points toward the bottom of the page.*)

Mrs. Jordan: Where?

Addie: On the feet!

Mrs. Jordan: Ah, so you started at the bottom of the page with the feet. What part are you working on next?

Addie: I need to do the pillow.

Mrs. Jordan: The pillow . . . and where does the pillow go?

Addie: (*Points under the bear.*) It has to go right there because the pillow is squished, but I ran out of room.

Mrs. Jordan: What do you mean you ran out of room?

Addie: I put the bear on the bottom, but the pillow is squished under the bear, so I ran out of room.

Mrs. Jordan: I see, and what are you trying to draw?

Addie: The bear, then the pillow, then the chair. And the pillow is squished under the bear.

Mrs. Jordan: That's right, the pillow is squished. It's squished between the bear and the chair. What do you think you might want to do now?

Addie: Can I start over?

Mrs. Jordan: Want to turn the paper over and try again?

Addie: Yeah . . . (*Turns the paper over and begins to put her pencil to the paper.*)

Mrs. Jordan: Wait, before you start drawing again, can you tell me your plan? What are you going to draw first?

Addie: The bear.

Mrs. Jordan: Okay, the bear. And where are you going to draw the bear? Are you going to draw it in the same place?

Addie: I'm going to draw it more up.

Mrs. Jordan: I think that's a good idea. That way, you have some more room for . . .

Addie: . . . the squished pillow and the chair.

In this interaction between Mrs. Jordan and Addie, they have now reached the last "describe" part of the Instructional Activity, where children can continue to describe spatial relationships as they talk about their drawings. Children might describe what they've drawn to each other, or they might have a conversation with the teacher—yet another opportunity to build from the powerful math within children's work.

Isn't it neat how much Addie uses the word *squished* throughout this exchange? *Squished* isn't thought of as a "math" word, but it is being used by Addie repeatedly because it helps her articulate her idea of where the pillow is in relation to the bear and the chair. This conversation supports Addie in outlining her plan to represent objects in relation to each other.

Questions from Teachers About Describe-Draw-Describe

Describe-Draw-Describe seems like such a language-heavy activity. How do I find the time to frontload the vocabulary that children are going to need to participate in the activity, especially for dual language learners?

This Instructional Activity does involve helping children to build different ways of articulating spatial relationships, and conversations may surface terms that are unfamiliar to children. It is important, however, to keep in mind that the starting point is always children's ideas. Children begin to make sense of new words and ideas by engaging with them in the context of the activity and in combination with gestures, movement, and other words they already know. Rather than worrying about children needing vocabulary ahead of time, anticipate the variety of ways children might begin to communicate their ideas and consider how your responses might enrich their mathematical language during the activity and beyond. Consider these tips:

- **Invite children to participate in whatever way makes sense to them.** There are a lot of ways to communicate ideas—verbal and nonverbal—so make sure children feel supported to share ideas they are excited or wondering about, point and gesture, agree with the idea of another child, and so on. A space that values participation in a variety of forms scaffolds engagement and allows for many different ideas to be put on the table.

- **Support children to voice their ideas in their language of choice.** Just as you would in other situations (like counting out loud), make sure children feel encouraged to voice their ideas in languages other than English if this is what they know. Even if you do not speak the same language as a child,

revoicing what they say is a productive follow-up move to validate their contribution. Encouraging a child to "tell us more" or "show us again" can help leverage their linguistic resources and promote further participation as they elaborate on their ideas.

- **Consider offering mathematical language judiciously.** As children communicate their ideas, find strategic moments to connect mathematical language to their contributions. The terminology you introduce may or may not be taken up immediately, but over time, the connections among informal and formal language, gesture, and representation will support conceptual understanding of important spatial ideas.

Exploring Children's Thinking: Representing Spatial Relations

At first glance, some teachers might worry that this activity feels like a formal copying or tracing task that is not developmentally appropriate. However, Mrs. Jordan knows that Describe-Draw-Describe is much more open-ended than it may seem on the surface. She is very intentional about how she poses the task, and she knows she will circulate among and engage with the children regularly while they are drawing. She follows up on what children say and do to help them see that this is just another way for them to share their ideas—this time, not just through language but also through written representation, which is another form of nonverbal communication and an essential mathematical practice. Mrs. Jordan knows she has time for just a couple minutes with Addie because she also wants to see what the other children are doing, but she first takes a moment to reflect upon their interaction.

It is so interesting to Mrs. Jordan that Addie chooses to start her drawing with the bear's feet because, in the past, Addie has typically started by drawing the head of a person or animal. She remembers, however, that Addie had a lot to say about the bear's feet earlier during the story reading—how they were up in the air, how they were probably stinky and maybe the mouse could smell them. Mrs. Jordan wonders if maybe Addie just really likes the way the bear's feet look and thus chooses to start drawing there. As seen in the interaction, Addie soon realizes that while feet usually touch the ground (the bottom of the paper), putting them there and drawing the bear along the bottom of the page results in not having enough room to include the pillow and the chair. When Addie wants to start her representation over on the back of the page, Mrs. Jordan encourages her to articulate what she might do differently this time. Addie says she will "draw it more up," meaning that she would start her drawing in a different position, higher up on the page, giving her another opportunity to manage the placement and relationships among the other components she wants to draw. Her finished representation, with the mouse to the left and the bear sitting on a pillow and a chair to the right, can be seen on page 40.

After spending a few minutes with Addie, Mrs. Jordan continues to circulate the room. She observes how children are making and revising their decisions about what to represent first, both where and how, and how to manage drawing other objects in relation to those already drawn. She is impressed at Oliver's perseverance in attempting multiple versions of the flashing arrow sign that appears on one page, always connecting the legs of the sign to the bottom of the page as the "ground," and rotating the paper to change its orientation and give him more "ground" to work with. She also notes Janely's ability to manage all three main components of the page—the sign, the mouse, and the bear—and include much detail (e.g., the leaves on top of the pear, the legs on the sign) while keeping track of objects' relative locations, differences in size, and orientations (e.g., the bear leaning back in the chair). Their drawings can also be seen on page 40.

Representing Spatial Relations

As children engage in drawing (representing) their ideas about spatial relations, make note of how they represent

- Objects (e.g., sign, blanket, jar)
- Details of objects (e.g., lights around the sign, leaves on the pear, blades of grass)
- Objects in relation to other objects (e.g., a boy on top of the diving board, a butterfly inside of the jar, a father crouching next to his son)
- Relative size (e.g., the bear takes up more space than the mouse, the trees in the background are smaller than the tree in the foreground)
- Orientation (e.g., an upside-down box, an arrow pointing up and to the right, a leaning bear)

While some ideas may build on each other, other discussions might encourage different ideas to surface.

Finished representations of the illustration from *There's a Bear on My Chair* (seen on page 36) from Addie (top), Oliver (bottom left), and Janely (bottom right).

The Young Child and Mathematics, Third Edition

Assessing Children's Understanding

Giving children plenty of opportunities to share their ideas through multiple forms of communication (e.g., informal and formal language, gesture, gaze, movement, representation) supports a range of participation and allows early childhood educators to learn a great deal about the details of children's understandings of spatial relations. Throughout this multifaceted Instructional Activity, children continue to articulate and extend their spatial reasoning while engaging with each other and the teacher around a children's storybook. As you read through the vignette, what did you notice about children's understandings of spatial relations?

We authors were privileged to watch Mrs. Jordan spend time in two different classrooms and had an opportunity to talk with her about what she noticed afterward. She sat down and flipped through the stack of finished drawings and shared the following with us:

> I love seeing all of the details that [children] put into their drawings. The lights around the sign, the cord, the bear's toes . . . oh, and the leaves on the pear. It was so interesting how they wanted to keep talking about the leaves on the pear. Or a mango, since so many of them thought it looks like a mango, which I can totally see. I see green on top. The leaf is green! And that leaf showed up in so many of the drawings. It's such an interesting detail, even if they only drew the mouse and pear and nothing else. And of course, they wanted to go get a green crayon—which sometimes we do use crayons—but today I just wanted to have pencil and paper for the drawings.

Mrs. Jordan continued to flip through drawings, sometimes pausing to rotate one and look at it more closely. She went on:

> I'm so glad I chose to focus on this page because there's three main parts: the sign, the mouse, and the bear. It gave the children more to pay attention to in terms of where they're going to put things and how they would space them out on the page, and I was impressed. So many of them were drawing at least two things side by side and able to show the different sizes. See? The sign on the left, the mouse on the right. Here's a mouse in the middle, and

the bear is huge on the right. Oh, and they have been getting so much better at using the whole page to do the scene, even if they don't draw all of the objects. When we first started doing this, you'd get stuff squished in one corner or they would draw one thing that took up the whole page. Now it's like they are getting better at stepping back and thinking about the whole spread—it's actually across two pages in the book if you look at it—and planning out where each piece would need to go so the whole scene fit on the page.

We also listened to Mrs. Jordan explain how glad she was that she got to talk to so many children while they were drawing:

> They had so much they wanted to tell me. That's what's fun about the drawing part of this activity and what I hope teachers will get out of doing this in their classrooms. Sometimes teachers get anxious about the drawing part, but when they [actually get to it], they realize that children have so much more to say. Of course, children build on what was said during the group conversation, but as they're drawing and as you ask those good questions—"Tell me about this part of your drawing," "Where did you start your drawing?," "What do you want to do next?"—you get to hear so much more about their ideas. It's like the act of drawing keeps encouraging them to tell you more. I can't wait until they have a little more experience with this, and then the teachers can get the children to share about their drawings with each other. I see a lot more of that later in the year and in the older grades.

Finally, since we overheard Mrs. Jordan discussing possible next steps with the classroom teachers, we wanted to know what they might do next to build on the details of children's spatial reasoning ideas. One teacher said she wanted to try this Instructional Activity out with a storybook that the children were already familiar with, since the book Mrs. Jordan read was new to them. Her goal was to find book page that featured multiple objects that children would have to attend to, perhaps one that had more of a foreground and background with different opportunities for perspective. Another teacher wanted to stick with the same book, so Mrs. Jordan said she might encourage teachers to try another page, like the one where the mouse is jumping out of the box (in his underwear!) since the element of movement gives children a different kind of opportunity to represent.

Observing and debriefing with Mrs. Jordan this way gave us an opportunity to document much of the complex, intertwined work of an early childhood educator as they plan instruction, reflect on in-the-moment assessment, review children's work, and support children in building on their own ideas. The combination of Mrs. Jordan's interactions with children, her post-activity reflection, and her conversations with teachers about possible next steps contributes to meaningful assessment with children's thinking at the center.

Spatial Relations in Informal Spaces

As you observe children throughout the day using a mathematical lens, it might feel as if children are engaged in geometry and spatial reasoning in almost everything that they are doing. They are constantly engaged in movement through and navigation of space as they move their bodies from one place to another, and they are regularly managing where something is in relation to something else.

While reading through these interactions, consider the following:

> What are the children doing?

> What spatial reasoning ideas are children engaging with in each space?

> What are children communicating (verbally and nonverbally)?

During Transitions

Children are on the rug for circle time, their bodies seated closely together around the rug's edge. Soon, it's time for them to head to different parts of the room for center time. At the different centers, they navigate among the other children in a small area as their bodies huddle around the different activities and materials. When center time is over, the children form a line at the door with one child standing directly behind another, getting ready to head outside; when it's time to head back inside, they form a similar line (maybe even in the same order) outside the classroom door. After washing their hands, they meander to the rug with a chosen storybook in hand. Once it's time for large group time again, they quickly reach over one another to find an empty spot on the shelf for the books they hold, rotating the book upright before placing it on the shelf between two other books. Then they head back to the rug to pick a spot to sit.

During Choice Time

In their chosen areas, children work with materials and manage how they are taken out, used, and put away. They reach behind the easel to get a new piece of paper for a painting. After they're finished, they hold the artwork flat across both hands to place it onto an empty tray of the drying rack. They crouch down in front of the bottom shelf of the block area and reach into nooks and crannies, retrieving all the wooden blocks they want to use to build their castle. When it's time to clean up, they figure out how to put away all of the blocks again so that they fit back perfectly on the bottom shelf. They choose the heaviest bin of pretend food items and need two children to carry the bin together to the dramatic play area and lift it onto the table. After they finish playing grocery store, they put all of the items back into the bin and return it to its place.

During Outdoor Time

Children are scattered on and around the outdoor play structure, climbing over it, crouching under it, making their way up the ladder, then down the slide before going back around to the steps again. Across the rest of the playground, children ride bikes and pull wagons, sometimes in a straight line back and forth and sometimes around a curvy track, making sure they don't crash into one another or the structure. Two children are kicking a ball back and forth, trying to decide how far apart they should stand. Other children play movement games where they follow each other, spread out across the whole playground as far as possible, or need to make sure their individual activities (like Hula-Hooping) don't interfere with another child's space.

As early childhood educators observe children across scenes like these, they might find moments to interact with children to highlight, enrich, and deepen children's mathematical engagement, all embedded within children's daily activities and play. They might even leverage some of these informal spaces to build on and connect to other classroom activities. Imagine Mrs. Jordan, for example, asking Utisah to describe the movements in the game he is playing with Addie on the play structure. Look back through the vignettes described in this section and consider this question: *How might an early childhood educator briefly interact with children to elicit and build on their spatial reasoning ideas?* Even without a teacher present, however, it is clear that children are engaging in and learning mathematics throughout the day.

Conclusion

Spatial relations do not seem to get as much attention as other early math content, but research suggests that engaging children in this work is critically important. Opportunities to explore and enrich children's understandings of spatial relations exist across a variety of spaces. These opportunities are particularly powerful when they stem from children's interactions with each other and with the environment—as children talk, play, climb, move, draw, and gesture—as well as when children step back from their work and rethink their plans. How might you engage the whole child as you support building understanding of spatial relations?

The Mathematics of Spatial Relations

by Linda M. Platas

The domain of geometry—the mathematics of shape and space—has long been a neglected younger sibling of number and operations in the family of mathematics. We pay attention to it, but frequently in an unintentional and superficial way (e.g., "Let's cut the cheese into triangles for the math activity today"). We ask children to identify stereotypical shapes and we use terms like *on top of* and *under* in circle time and book reading. One could argue that not only are we underestimating the considerable contributions of geometric thinking in children's lives now and in the future, but we are also underestimating children's interest in a fascinating world of shape and space, a world full of interesting ideas and applications.

Geometric thinking provides tools to understand physical attributes of the space we inhabit and the things within it. Children use geometric thinking to solve problems through manipulation (both mental and real) of objects and representations of those objects in their environments. In the process, they notice important geometrical patterns and relationships. These next sections describe important aspects of the mathematics of shape and space.

The Vocabulary of Shape and Space

In order to adequately support children's learning, teachers need to think about fostering both geometric language *and* concepts. Research has shown that the amount of spatial language that caregivers (e.g., parents, relatives, teachers) use in their interactions with children, and children's own use of this vocabulary in turn, helps children categorize objects and spatial relationships based on their perceptions (e.g., *on* as an indication that an object is supported or attached, such as "*on* the table" or "*on* your jacket") and understand the real world around them. Providing an environment that is rich with spatial vocabulary can call attention to the attributes of objects themselves and

their position in space. Spatial language includes words describing location/position (*under, in front of*); attributes (*long, high, side, angle, same, symmetrical*); orientation and mental transformation (*left, turn, match*); and geometric shape names (*rectangular prism, triangle, sphere*).

Spatial Relations

Spatial relations are simply the relationships of objects in space. This includes the relationship of these objects to one another and their relationship to ourselves. An infant's first interactions with the world are explorations of the spatial relationships within their environment. As children gain more experience moving and interacting in a variety of environments, their navigation and manipulation (gross and fine motor) skills improve. Children learn to throw balls through basketball hoops (albeit short ones!), draw pictures of their homes and siblings, and position blocks to create castles.

Geometric Figures

We do a lot of shape naming in our classrooms. We put shapes on our walls (e.g., shape posters), we point them out in the environment (e.g., doors, balls), and we ask children to draw them and cut them out. In reality, teaching children the names of shapes is a mixed bag. Children typically learn to recognize prototypical shapes (e.g., an isosceles triangle pointed up), but they do not learn that, more formally, shapes are classified according to rules and definitions (e.g., triangles are closed figures with three angles and three straight sides and are triangles regardless of their position; pyramids are named after their bases, and triangular bases result in triangular pyramids while square bases result in square pyramids). When we try to teach children these rules, we open ourselves to unexpected complexities. Is the window frame really a rectangle? After all, it is a three-dimensional object, not a two-dimensional object.

And are the corners really right angles? (Generally, after time and a few paint jobs, the corners have a bit of a curve to them!) How do we handle these questions from ourselves and the children we teach? Teachers need to break out the honesty: "This looks like a rectangle to me, but what do rectangles have to have? Does this window frame have all of those attributes?" Imagine what kind of conversations and deep understanding this can support in the classroom.

Knowledge of shape attributes contributes to children's ability to compose shapes (e.g., putting two congruent right triangles together to create a rectangle; putting two congruent right triangular prisms together to create a rectangular prism) and decompose them (e.g., the reverse of composition actions). These two abilities further contribute to children's skills in physical and mental transformations, described next.

Physical and Mental Transformations

Let's get back to more familiar ground: puzzles. Supporting children's development in physical and mental transformations has become a hot topic due to recent research that has found a strong relationship between these skills in early childhood and mathematics achievement in the fields of science, technology, engineering, and mathematics (STEM). Young children's manipulations involving composing and decomposing shapes and manipulating puzzle pieces provide opportunities to develop their skills in transforming (sliding, flipping, turning) shapes and objects both in the physical world and mentally. Initially, children might try to fit a puzzle piece by placing it where they think it goes and turning it until it fits (or doesn't). Later, children can look at puzzle pieces on the table and, by rotating pieces in their mind, imagine which one can be turned to fit an available spot on the puzzle. Children can do the same thing with tangrams, thinking ahead of time about which shapes might go together in which ways to create a particular figure (e.g., ship, house).

What Comes First?

The geometric and spatial concepts explored here are all within children's reach. There is no "first step." Teachers should feel free to expose children to all of these ideas and provide rich language and physical environments that support this important area of development.

For more about young children's spatial relations learning, visit the DREME TE Project's website at https://prek-math-te.stanford.edu.

Adapted, with permission, from L.M. Platas, "The Mathematics of Geometry and Spatial Relations," *DREME TE Project* (Stanford, CA: Stanford University, DREME Network, 2017).

CHAPTER 3
Measurement and Data

Children naturally notice and collect information about their world. Tall buildings, tiny ants, heavy backpacks, and loud motorcycles draw their excitement and wonder. Children use what they notice to make decisions, reason, and ask questions ("It's cold, so I'm going to wear my jacket," "If I go down that hill on my bike, I will go really fast!"). They attend to similarities and differences between people, places, and objects and begin to communicate about the attributes and relations that draw their attention ("That slide is really, really, big," "Your banana is littler than mines," "My dad is more bigger than your grandpa").

This chapter explores young children's engagement with measurement and data. *Measurement* is about quantifying particular kinds of attributes, such as length, weight, and volume—or even time, temperature, and sound. *Data* is about gathering, organizing, examining, and summarizing information.

The observations and comparisons children inherently make on a daily basis provide entry points to make sense of important ideas about measurement and data. Supporting the development of children's understandings of these ideas requires listening to what children notice; supporting them in communicating their experiences and observations; and helping them begin to systematically compare, reason, and ask questions about their collective noticings.

We begin by exploring measurement in Ms. Torres's classroom in two different informal spaces that you might recognize as a regular part of your day. Later, Ms. Recinos will engage her preschoolers in an Instructional Activity called What Do You Notice? across two different days, and we will observe how she shifts the math focus to first highlight measurement and then data with the same activity.

Measurement and Data in Informal Spaces

Building a House During Work Time in Ms. Torres's Classroom

The children in Ms. Torres's preschool classroom are engrossed in work time. During work time, children select an activity or area of the classroom in which to explore, create, or play together. There are numerous materials and spaces available to choose from. Several children are in the kitchen area "making lunch." Christopher and Luis are building a garage for toy cars out of blocks, while Samuel and Mia paint at an easel. Valerie, Carlos, and Jacqueline are dressing up as animals.

Nearby, Samantha picks up the basket of Magna-Tiles. After dumping a pile of tiles onto the carpet, she begins to build a house by putting square tiles together and making a cube. Ms. Torres sits down and watches for several moments as Samantha puts more tiles on top of the cube, extending the tower upward. Samantha begins to tell her teacher about what she is doing.

Samantha: The house is really nice.

Ms. Torres: The house is really nice?

Samantha: And tall.

Ms. Torres: Oh, okay. So, are you going to build the house taller (*Gestures up with her hands.*) or are you going to build the house wider (*Spreads her hands apart.*)?

Samantha: (*Continues building but does not respond verbally.*)

Ms. Torres: Hmm. Are you going to go up? (*Points upward with her finger.*)

Samantha: Yeah.

Ms. Torres: Yeah? You're going to build it taller?

Samantha: Yeah.

Here, we see ideas about length emerge in the context of play. When Samantha describes her house as "tall," Ms. Torres picks up on this idea by introducing comparative terms (e.g., *taller, wider*) and linking them with gestures to show how the house is changing. At first, Samantha does not take up her teacher's question. Rather than pressing for a response, Ms. Torres asks her question in a different way, allowing Samantha to agree, and then restates the idea using the word "taller."

Ms. Torres: Oh my goodness. Are you going to have a kitchen?

A few minutes later, Priscilla, who is much taller than Samantha, approaches and asks if she can join in with the house-building.

Priscilla: Samantha, can I play?

Samantha: Yeah.

Ms. Torres: Samantha, tell Priscilla how you're building your house.

Samantha: The house is really big.

Ms. Torres: The house is going to be very big, huh?

Priscilla: Can I help?

Samantha: (*Nods.*)

Ms. Torres: Samantha told me she wants to build her house taller. (*Gestures upward.*) She wants to make it go up. So, how tall is your house going to be, Samantha?

Samantha: Really big.

Ms. Torres: Is it going to be taller than you?

Samantha: Yeah.

Ms. Torres: Or taller than, um . . .

Priscilla: Priscilla!

Ms. Torres: Priscilla?

Samantha: Taller than Priscilla.

Ms. Torres: Taller than Priscilla? Oh wow! Stand up, let me see how tall you are.

Priscilla: (*Stands.*)

Ms. Torres: Wow. Are you going to make the house taller than Priscilla?

Samantha: (*Smiles and nods.*)

Priscilla: But I'm big, I'm four.

⋯⋯ While Ms. Torres sees an opportunity to engage Samantha in talk related to measurement, she also recognizes the importance of keeping the conversation grounded in play. This question (about if the house is going to have a kitchen) helps to return the focus to house-building and Samantha as the driver of the activity.

⋯⋯ Notice the subtle shift here in what is being asked. So far, we have moved from a descriptive term (tall), to a comparative term (taller). Now, the phrasing *how tall* invites other ways to talk about height, which might include amounts of different kinds of units, such as square tiles, centimeters, inches, or Samanthas!

Priscilla and Samantha continue to build their house higher and higher. A few minutes later, their house is over 10 Magna-Tile cubes tall! Ms. Torres notices that they are about to run out of Magna-Tiles and decides to ask the girls about their progress.

Ms. Torres: The house is getting pretty tall, huh?

Samantha: Yeah!

Ms. Torres: Let me see, Samantha. Do you want to stand up? Let's see if it's taller than you.

Samantha: (*Stands.*)

Ms. Torres: Who's taller? Samantha or the house?

Samantha: Me! I'm taller!

Ms. Torres: Wow, you're taller than the house! What about Priscilla? Let's see, Priscilla.

Priscilla: (*Stands.*)

Ms. Torres: Now who's taller?

Priscilla: Me.

Ms. Torres: Okay, so who's smaller?

Samantha: Me.

Ms. Torres: The house, Samantha, or Priscilla?

Priscilla: Um, Samantha.

Ms. Torres: Samantha.

Samantha: I'm much smaller.

Ms. Torres: (*Nods.*) Mm-hmm, Samantha is smaller than Priscilla. How about the house? Is the house taller than Samantha?

Priscilla: Um . . . um, downer. (*Gestures down with her hand.*)

Ms. Torres: Yeah, the house is down below Samantha. It's shorter than Samantha.

Samantha: I win!

Priscilla: I win too!

Ms. Torres: You win? Why do you win?

Priscilla: Because, um, we're taller!

••••••• Samantha and Priscilla, like many young children, are successful in performing *direct comparisons*—comparing one thing to another in terms of a particular attribute. The comparisons are more complicated here as the relative height of three things is being compared from both directions (taller and smaller).

••••••• Priscilla is taking a step toward becoming more precise with her language. Rather than using the more general term of *smaller*, she describes smaller as related to height by motioning with her hand and saying "downer." Recognizing this advance in understanding, Ms. Torres picks up on Priscilla's word and connects it to another height-specific term: *shorter*.

To watch a video featuring Ms. Torres engaging with Samantha and Priscilla as they build with Magna-Tiles, scan this code or visit https://prek-math-te.stanford.edu/measurement-data/classroom-videos-measurement-data.

In the context of creative play, Samantha, Priscilla, and Ms. Torres explore several interrelated aspects of measurement. They work to focus their conversation about making the house "bigger" toward a particular attribute related to measuring length: height. They perform several direct comparisons, comparing how tall Samantha and Priscilla are to one another and to the house. They extend and elaborate on their initial comparisons by examining height relations from different perspectives: Priscilla is taller than Samantha, Samantha is smaller than Priscilla. In doing so, they also take a step toward greater precision, moving from a general measurement term (*smaller*) to one intended to specifically convey lesser height (*downer*). Throughout, Ms. Torres plays a critical role in supporting each child's reasoning and communication by eliciting their ideas, integrating language and gestures, and following up on their ideas when she affirms their observations and helps them to clarify what they mean.

The next vignette also takes place in Ms. Torres's classroom but on another day. Each morning, every child is provided with a breakfast that includes a small carton of milk. Watch as this group of children cleans up after breakfast time.

During Breakfast Cleanup

After breakfast, children pour their leftover milk into collection pitchers sitting in the middle of the table so that the milk can be poured down the drain rather than thrown into the already-heavy trash bags. Ms. Torres intentionally sets out a specific type of container for the children to use during this task—a measuring cup for liquids—and makes sure that it's available in a variety of sizes.

Julian really wants Evan to "put it in the small!" Evan, however, has a different plan. He aims for the larger container, the one that Julian already considers too full. Evan very slowly and carefully pours more milk until that container is filled to the brim before moving onto the empty container. He then triumphantly comments to Ms. Torres that he made "more work," as she will have to carry the container quite carefully to the sink.

After Evan finishes, it's Alexa's turn, and she adds her milk to the less full container. Soon all of the children have finished emptying their milk cartons, and the full pitchers are ready to be emptied into the sink.

By "put it in the small," Julian means that he wants Evan to pour his milk into the container that has a smaller amount (or lesser volume) of milk in it.

Reflection Question: What might children notice about the milk in the containers? How might you engage them in these observations? How could this support them in their developing notions of measurement?

The progression of the children in Ms. Torres's class emptying their milk cartons into different containers.

The Young Child and Mathematics, Third Edition

Instructional Activity: What Do You Notice?

Children *notice*. They notice color, texture, and size and compare similar things to one another. They like to tell you about what they notice. Finding ways to support children in talking about what they notice can create openings to work on math concepts, including measurement and data.

What Do You Notice? is an Instructional Activity that invites children to consider and communicate about a range of content. For this activity, the teacher typically displays an image, asks children to think silently about what they notice, and then invites them to engage in conversation about what they've noticed. By listening to and picking up on what children notice, teachers can draw out, extend, and connect children's ideas and support them in making sense of and building on one another's ideas. The following examples of this Instructional Activity in Ms. Recinos's preschool classroom illustrate ways you might elicit and explore children's ideas about measurement and data. Depending on the image, what captures children's interest, and the teacher's goal, this activity can also be used to seed conversations about spatial relations, numbers, patterns, and more.

Noticing Dogs in Ms. Recinos's Classroom

The children in Ms. Recinos's class have gathered on the carpet, all facing the blank white board. Ms. Recinos is ready to project an image of a group of different-sized dogs onto the board.

Ms. Recinos: Okay, everyone, I'm going to show you a picture, and I want you to look at it and think about what you notice. I'm going to ask you to think quietly to yourself so that everyone has plenty of time to look and think. Are you ready?

Children: Yes! (*Nod.*)

Ms. Recinos: All right, here we go. (*Reveals image of a group of different-sized dogs.*) Think silently to yourself. What do you notice?

Children: Ooh! Dogs! (*Several immediately raise their hands.*)

Ms. Recinos: Let's just look with our eyes for a minute. (*Smiles and motions for the children to put their hands down.*) Think to yourself about what you notice. See if you can come up with at least two ideas.

About a minute passes while children silently look at the image. Ms. Recinos sits down on the rug and looks at the image with them. She sees children gazing up and down and across the whole group of dogs. A couple of children begin to point at the dogs, gesturing first toward the bottom left then diagonally upwards to the right.

•••••••• While there are many things that children (and adults) might notice about the dogs in the photograph (seen on page 55), Ms. Recinos hopes to use it as a way of learning about the children's informal ideas about measurement. She is particularly interested in how they may communicate their ideas of *big* or *little* and compare the dogs in terms of their "bigness." She expects that some children will attend to the dogs' relative heights but is wondering if anyone will raise the notion of weight.

Ms. Recinos: Okay, I think we're ready to share with each other what we noticed. When you're ready, you can ask the person next to you about what they noticed. Go ahead.

There is a burst of excited chatter as the children turn and talk to one another about what they notice. Many point to the image and exclaim in enthusiasm as they listen and share. Ms. Recinos leans in to listen to Zayra and Alyssa's conversation. Alyssa is pointing to the dog near the middle, saying it has "pointy ears." Zayra points at the grey dog on the right and says, "That one's not in order. My grandma has a dog like that. It's so soft and I like to hug it." Nearby, Daniel gestures at the brown dog with a tilted head and leans his own head over to the side. His partner César says, "Oh yeah! Like this!" and mirrors Daniel's movement. Ms. Recinos then sees that Clarise, who rarely speaks, is smiling and talking with her partner. Ms. Recinos decides to call the class back together and calls on Clarise to begin the conversation.

> Ms. Recinos always makes sure to listen in and observe as children talk to each other. This is a prime opportunity for her to learn a lot about the range of ideas that might surface in the coming conversation and how children communicate about these ideas. She is particularly excited to see how the children are not just sharing their own noticings—they are also listening to and engaging with one another's ideas!

Ms. Recinos: I can't wait to hear what you noticed about our picture. Clarise, would you like to tell us what you noticed?

Clarise: Doggies.

Esmerelda: *¡Hay perritos!*

Ms. Recinos: *Si, hay perritos*—there are doggies. What did you notice about the doggies, Clarise?

Clarise: Mmm. . . . (*Pauses, then continues softly.*) Puppies.

Massimo: A chihuahua!

Ms. Recinos: Ah yes! Some of the dogs are puppies—

Massimo: (*Interjects.*) A chihuahua!

Ms. Recinos: —and one of them is a chihuahua. What else do you notice?

Jaya: That one looks like my dog.

Ms. Recinos: Yeah, one of them looks like my dog too.

Kierra: There's one, two, three, four, five, six.

Ms. Recinos: Okay, there's six dogs. What else do you notice?

Leo: There's big pippies.

Zayra: The grey one has a fluffy tail!

César: That one is sad. It's going like this. (*Tips his head to the side and frowns.*)

Ms. Recinos: That one does look sad. Leo, can you say that again?

> As usual, Ms. Recinos wants to elicit a wide range of children's ideas, but today, she is particularly interested in listening for and extending ideas related to size in terms of height and weight. With this in mind, she acknowledges Kierra's idea about counting the dogs but, in this moment, chooses to pursue other children's ideas.

The photo of different-sized dogs that Ms. Recinos shows the children.

Leo: There's big pippies!

Ms. Recinos: Oh, there's big puppies?

Camila: There's a little one.

Ms. Recinos: Some are big and some are little?

Children: Uh huh, yeah.

Victoria: There's different sizes.

Ms. Recinos: Hmm, okay. I wonder which one you think is the biggest.

Children: (*Many say "Ooh!" and raise their hands, including Sofía.*)

Ms. Recinos: Sofía, which one do you think is the biggest?

Sofía: That one. (*Points at the standing dog, at the far right.*)

Ms. Recinos: This one over here on the end? (*Points.*)

Sofía: Yes.

Ms. Recinos: What do other people think? Do you agree with Sofía that this dog on the right is the biggest?

Children: (*Many nod but several others, including Alyssa, shake their heads.*)

Ms. Recinos: Alyssa, what do you think?

Alyssa: The pointy ears dog is really, really big. But it's lying down.

Victoria: No, that one is the biggest. (*Points toward the dog with the tilted head.*)

Ms. Recinos is hoping to get some disagreement. She wants to explore different ways that children might think about what "biggest" could mean.

Ms. Recinos: Hmm, Victoria thinks the one that César says looks sad is the biggest.

Alyssa: No, I think the pointy ears one is bigger because look at its feet—it's lower.

Ms. Recinos: What do you mean it's lower?

Alyssa: 'Cause the sad one is sitting up higher. Like it's up on something, but we can't see it because of the little dog in front, the one with the fluffy tail.

Children: Oh, yeah!

Ms. Recinos: Okay, Alyssa says this one is a little bit higher in the picture than the one next to it. (*Gestures with her hand at the base of each dog, emphasizing that they are not level with each other.*) It kind of tricks us. Is that what you mean?

Alyssa: Yeah. And also, maybe it's a puppy.

Daniel: It's one year old. It's going to get taller.

Ms. Recinos: Oh, you think that one is going to get taller. What do you think, Sebastián?

Sebastián: I think that one there with pointy ears is the biggest.

Liam: Yeah, the one that's lying down and resting.

Ms. Recinos: This one, that's lying down?

Liam: Yeah, when it stands up, it will be taller.

Ms. Recinos: Is that what you were thinking, Sebastián?

Sebastián: No.

Ms. Recinos: No? Okay, what were you thinking?

Sebastián: Because it's too heavy for me.

Ms. Recinos: What do you mean?

Sebastián: It's too big. I can't pick it up. My dad could carry it, but I can't carry it.

Victoria: I could carry it—I'm super strong!

Ms. Recinos: Oh, okay. Sebastián thinks this one is the heaviest. It's too big to carry. That's an interesting idea. What do other people think about that?

César: *Mi tío* (my uncle) has a dog like that, and when he jumps up on me, he pushes me down.

Ms. Recinos: Yeah, sometimes a heavy dog might push us over. I wonder . . . are there any dogs that you think you *could* carry? That you could pick up?

Camila: That one, the little one.

While Alyssa's explanation (it is bigger because "it's lower") might be difficult to interpret, she is calling attention to an important idea—that comparing relative heights is complicated because the dogs do not share a common origin, or starting point, in the photograph; additionally, some dogs are lying down while others are sitting up. By asking Alyssa to say more about her explanation, the idea is elaborated on in a way that allows other children the opportunity to engage with her idea.

Liam extends Sebastián's idea by giving a reason why the dog with pointy ears might be "bigger."

By supporting the children's engagement and checking back with Sebastián, two different ideas are allowed to surface.

Kierra: The tiny one *and* the medium one.

Ms. Recinos: You could pick up both of those, Kierra? This dog here on the end and this one next to it? (*Points to dog on far left and the next in line, respectively.*)

Kierra: Uh-huh.

Ms. Recinos: Which one do you think is lighter? Which one would be easier to pick up?

Kierra: That one is more lighter. (*Points to dog on far left.*)

Lamar: That one is the heaviest and that one is the lightest!

Ms. Recinos: Oh wow. What else do you notice?

The conversation continues for several more minutes with children sharing ideas about the dogs' colors and the textures of their fur. There is also a brief debate about whether or not the dogs' ears should count when determining their height and which dogs might be puppies and become heavier when they're fully grown. Ms. Recinos is careful to strike a balance between picking up on the children's noticings related to height and weight (and age) and keeping the conversation moving to make sure that each child has a chance to share what they noticed.

Reflection Question: Looking back through the conversation, what did Ms. Recinos learn about the children's varied ideas about measurement?

Exploring Children's Thinking: Measurement

Though it might appear that Ms. Torres and Ms. Recinos are simply asking questions and inviting children to respond, a closer look reveals the different ways they draw on in-depth knowledge regarding how children think and talk about ideas related to measurement. Knowing what to look and listen for allows teachers to recognize and pick up on particular things children say and do to support the development of measurement understanding.

While children notice a lot of different things about their world, there are particular characteristics that are central to building concepts related to measurement. Making sense of measurement requires building understandings about the kinds of attributes that can be measured. When Ms. Torres asks Samantha if she is going to build her house taller or wider, she offers ways of thinking about and describing length (a measurement of distance in one direction). Had their conversation played out differently, perhaps focusing on how much space on the carpet the house would take up or how many rooms the house would have, they might have instead explored Samantha's ideas related to area (a two-dimensional measurement of surface)

or capacity (a three-dimensional measurement of space). Relatedly, when Ms. Recinos asks the children which dog they think is the biggest and elicits *why* each child thinks a particular dog is the biggest, she helps children to make explicit different ways of conceptualizing size. Is the "biggest" dog the tallest one? The longest? The heaviest? Unpacking what children mean when they use words like *big* and *small* is an early step in learning about and distinguishing between concepts of height, weight, volume, and even time. For some children, "bigger" often means older (and it's confusing when an older person is shorter)!

As children attend to and discern between different attributes, they also begin to compare things to one another. Children are naturally quite good at making direct comparisons (that is, comparing one thing to another in terms of a particular attribute). It is important to note that when children make comparisons and use words like *bigger, taller,* and *older,* they often include the subject but omit the referent. For example, when Samantha compares herself to the house and says, "I'm taller!," she does not name the thing to which she is being compared: the house. When Ms. Torres restates Samantha's observation ("You're taller than the house"), and later when she nudges the girls to clarify what they

mean ("The house, Samantha, or Priscilla?"), she is helping them make their thinking explicit in terms of the referent. Switching the subject and referent in a comparison changes its direction, and therefore the term used to describe the relationship. Sometimes children know the term that describes a greater amount (e.g., *taller, heavier*) but don't yet know the corresponding term if the direction of the comparison is reversed (e.g., *shorter, lighter*). Young children's inventiveness can be a powerful resource in these moments. When Ms. Torres asks "Is the house taller than Samantha?" and Priscilla responds with "downer," she shows that she knows the situation calls for a more specific word than *smaller* and uses her knowledge of *up* and *down* to create a word that means less height. Encouraging this sensemaking and creativity is important in supporting children's understandings of how making comparisons works.

Over time, children extend their understandings of the kinds of things that can be measured and what matters when making comparisons. As they continue to make sense of length, weight, capacity, and so on, they begin to see how these attributes can be quantified; in other words, rather than just being *tall* or *heavy*, you can have a certain amount of "tallness" or "heaviness." However, unlike discrete sets of objects (e.g., rocks, toy cars), measuring continuous quantities involves parsing them into units of certain amounts, such as inches or gallons. In extending

their understandings of comparisons, children come to see how making multiple direct comparisons can allow them to make claims about and order a set of things according to a measurable attribute, sometimes referred to as *seriation*. They also notice that making comparisons is much easier when the things being compared have a shared origin, or common starting point. When Alyssa notices that the "sad" dog with the tilted head is sitting up higher than the dog to the left of it, she is attending to this idea. The children are also working to make sense of where to start and end measuring when they question whether or not the dogs' ears should count toward their heights. This also happens when, for example, children compare their heights and someone stands on their toes.

Bringing these ideas together allows children to perform and reason about measurements. Through experiences measuring various things in their world, children begin to develop a sense of how much an inch, meter, gallon, pound, or hour is, and thus the kinds of tools that might be useful in a given situation. Measuring objects also allows for indirect comparisons, where the relationship between two things can be determined by their relationship to a third thing. For example, a child might compare the height of a table inside the classroom with one out on the playground by measuring each height in terms of where the table touches their own body or with a tool such as a measuring tape.

The Mathematics of Measurement

by Linda M. Platas

This chapter overviews important concepts that children learn as they engage in measurement activities, including comparing, ordering three or more objects, origin, and nonstandard and standard measurement. Gaining an understanding of these concepts allows children to accurately and meaningfully measure objects and environments by the attributes (dimensions or properties) that they are interested in. These attributes are described next.

Length and Height

Length and height are linear measurements and are perhaps the most commonly measured in early childhood activities. They can be measured by both nonstandard and standard measurement tools. Children's understanding of length develops over an extended period of time (well into the primary school years) and includes, but is not limited to, the concepts of origin and unit, attribute (length has a beginning and an end), and conservation (like number, if nothing is added or taken away, the length does not change regardless of position).

Area

Children informally use area measurement all the time ("You have more room in the sandbox than I do! Look, I don't have any room for my legs"). Area can be more complicated to measure than length because it is two-dimensional (by contrast, height and length are one-dimensional), so children need to pay attention to two attributes at the same time: width and length. Children can measure area with square tiles, placing them end to end and adjacent, or they can make use of graph paper. Measuring area with standard measurement tools, such as rulers or measuring tapes, requires multiplication and is generally explored later in the primary school years.

Capacity

Water tables, sandboxes, cooking activities, and mealtimes offer rich opportunities for the measurement of capacity, or the amount a container can hold. In water and sand tables, both nonstandard (e.g., dump trucks, teacups, buckets) and standard (e.g., measuring cups with or without graduated units) measuring tools are useful and engaging to children. Children explore capacities of cups during mealtimes, especially if they are allowed to pour their own beverages. Recipes provide excellent classroom activities that use both number and measurement. This can include nonconsumables like playdough or hot and cold consumables like smoothies and quick breads.

Weight

The measurement of weight is another common classroom activity. Children frequently use their hands to compare the weights of two objects. Balance scales provide nonnumerical comparisons of two objects, and spring (or digital) scales add number to those comparisons. Children can learn to differentiate weight from size by experimenting with large, light objects (such as Styrofoam blocks) and small, heavy objects (like metal blocks).

Time

Standard time measurement is a very difficult concept for children to grasp in preschool and kindergarten. Our formal division of time (60 seconds in a minute; 60 minutes in an hour; 24 hours in a day; 7 days in a week; 28, 29, 30, or 31 days in a month; 12 months in a year!) is idiosyncratic and may be confusing to a child. A good place to start teaching about time measurement is with the vocabulary of time. Words like *morning*, *afternoon*, *evening*, *night*, *day*, *tomorrow*, *yesterday, after,* and *before* can provide a foundation for later time concepts. Children can also take turns making

use of hourglasses and timers in the classroom. It is important to use accurate terminology with regard to time. For instance, stating that you'll be back in a few minutes when you are going on a lunch hour provides an inaccurate statement of time to a child. Although use of the calendar during circle or whole group time is common, its seemingly arbitrary structure makes it less useful than other activities in supporting mathematical development.

Temperature

As with time, formal measurement of temperature can be difficult for young children to understand. This is particularly true if children live in areas where there aren't a wide range of temperatures. When it is hot in the summer and snowing in the winter, temperature takes on a bit more meaning!

As with time, introducing temperature words and their meanings as a foundation for later understanding of temperature can be useful. These terms include *hot*, *warm*, *cool*, *cold*, *freezing*, and *boiling*.

For more about young children's measurement learning, visit the DREME TE Project's website at https://prek-math-te.stanford.edu.

Adapted, with permission, from L.M. Platas, "The Mathematics of Measurement," *DREME TE Project* (Stanford, CA: Stanford University, DREME Network, 2018).

A Fruit Survey by Ms. Recinos's Class

The following week, Ms. Recinos asks the children to select their favorite fruit from a list with pictures. Each child makes a mark on the paper using a black marker. She also makes some marks using a blue marker, one in the strawberries category for herself and two in the grapes category for her teaching partner and the preschool director.

Ms. Recinos decides to use the same What Do You Notice? activity as a way of presenting the results of the survey to the class and engaging them in a conversation about analyzing data.

Clarise notices that three people (including her) chose bananas, and several children want to share which fruit they chose. Kevin says that "Actually my favorite fruit is mango," but since that wasn't an option, he chose strawberries instead. Marcus notices the blue marks and asks about them. When Ms. Recinos says that those marks represent the grown-ups' choices, the class insists on her telling them which grown-up chose what fruit.

Camila is disappointed that oranges "lost" since they are her favorite, but she is excited to find out that the other person who chose oranges is her friend Bethany. Jeremiah comments that there are "a lot" of strawberries and grapes but only one apple, one banana, and one orange in the pictures on the survey results. Vanessa says that strawberries were chosen by the most people; Alyssa disagrees.

Ms. Recinos asks the class which fruit they think most people here like. Some children say strawberries, a few say apples, and a few others say both. Daniel says, "I don't know." Ms. Recinos asks him what he's thinking about, and he says that the marks are kind of bunched together, so it's hard to tell. Ms. Recinos invites him to come up and count the marks, and they determine that both apples and strawberries were chosen by six people. César says, "Yeah but if it was only kids, then apples would win."

Victoria decides that she wants to switch her choice from grapes to oranges so that oranges can have the same number of marks as bananas. Sebastián reminds Ms. Recinos that Leo has been absent the past two days, so he didn't get a chance to vote. Ms. Recinos asks the class to share their predictions about what fruit they think Leo might choose and why.

In contrast to the previous example, where Ms. Recinos chose a preexisting image of different-sized dogs that she thought would interest the children and tap into their intuitive ideas about measurement, here she uses a data representation that the class has created together. This data representation is the focus for another What Do You Notice? activity, this one centered on data.

Since the children have made their own tick marks on the fruit survey, you might notice that they are a bit "messy" and the spacing between the marks varies. This can complicate the work of making relative comparisons, but it also provides an opportunity to consider differences between space and quantity. And perhaps more importantly, children get to see that there is a specific mark that is just for them.

Results of the Favorite Fruit Survey by Ms. Recinos's Class

Favorite Fruit	How Many People?
Apple / *Manzana*	| | | / | |
Banana / *Plátano*	(| |
Strawberries / *Fresas*	(| | | | |
Orange / *Naranja*	| |
Grapes / *Uvas*	| | | | |

Questions from Teachers About What Do You Notice?

What Do You Notice? seems like such an open-ended activity. How can I make sure I am working toward my mathematical goals?

This activity is designed with a focus on participation first; every child should feel invited to the conversation in a way that works for them. You may wonder how to encourage many different children to share their noticings while also making sure to surface and follow up on important math that emerges. Digging too much into every idea might cause the conversation to stall. However, selectively asking children to elaborate on an idea or respond to a peer's noticings can nudge the conversation toward particular mathematical goals. Here are some tips for how to navigate the balance of making this activity open yet intentional:

- **Use different kinds of images.** Some images might provide richer opportunities for particular math ideas over others. Some entice you to count a lot of pumpkins, while others might draw your eyes to curved roadways and long shadows. You might even want to revisit an image you discussed previously to elicit and build on different ideas.

- **Anticipate what children might notice and talk about.** Take a moment to consider in advance ideas that are likely to surface during the conversation with children. Use what you know about your group of children and their experiences as you anticipate. (This is also a great way to collaborate and plan with a colleague.) Doing so will allow you to think about the variety of follow-up responses you might provide.

- **Consider more than one possible mathematical goal.** Have a few questions ready that might build on particular math ideas. Sometimes you may think an image will lend itself to specific math content (e.g., comparing heights, conceptualizing large quantities), but children may take the conversation in other, equally worthy directions (e.g., making shapes from other shapes, describing movement). Having a plan is helpful, but you may revise your plan when children surprise you with their curiosity and creativity!

Exploring Children's Thinking: Data

Children love to ask questions. They also love to notice things that are similar and group them together. Wondering about who is absent today, reporting their favorite TV shows, and putting toy vehicles into a line of cars and a line of trucks are all things that come naturally to children. They are also early ways of engaging in processes related to gathering and organizing data. Supporting children in making sense of data can begin by leveraging their curiosity and inclination to sort and group objects and information.

It can be quite powerful for children to see themselves in data. Collecting survey data about children's lives, interests, and preferences can help them to see data as related to themselves and the people in their world. For example, you might survey children about their pets, number of siblings, or favorite food (as Ms. Recinos did). Children might even design their own survey and collect information from their peers. It is also powerful for children to formulate questions that might be answered through observing their world; for example, "Do more children walk to school, drive, or take the bus?," "What do my classmates choose to do during choice time?," or "Who does the most laps on the bike path during outside time?" The observational data that results from gathering answers to these questions mines children's natural curiosity and allows them to see themselves as data producers, rather than just consumers.

An eventual goal in learning about data is to see how it can be used to answer questions that are not immediately obvious. For example, the question "How can we make our school drop-off area safer?" opens opportunities to collect data about cars stopping at the stop sign in front of the school (e.g., who stops and who doesn't, what the busiest times of the day are, if there are any adults watching to make sure that people stop, defining what counts as a stop). Learning to collect, organize, and make sense of the resulting data can even provide an entry point into taking collective action in children's local community.

That said, many children need to be able to make sense of data in relation to themselves before they can step back and reason about the entire representation. During the fruit survey in Ms. Recinos's class, for example, Clarise, Kevin, and Camila make meaning of the data in relation to their own particular choices. By collecting, organizing, and representing particular information, children can begin to consider different kinds of questions and the corresponding data that might be used to answer such questions.

After data has been gathered, children can create or examine data displays to notice frequencies, see relationships, and even make predictions. For example, when Camila says that the oranges "lost," she is noticing the relative frequency of oranges to other fruit. Similarly, when the class has some difficulty determining which fruit was chosen by the most people, some may be grappling with the idea that what matters in the representation is the number of marks in the right column, not the size of the marks or the amount of space they take up on the chart. Jeremiah, in noticing the amount of each fruit shown in the pictures on the chart, may also be working out what aspects of the data representation provide what kinds of information.

An important goal is not just learning to read and represent data displays but also developing a critical lens through which to consider what is represented *and* what might be left out. Embedded within César's idea that "if it was only kids, then apples would win" are important issues related to sampling and parsing data. Relatedly, Kevin's comment about mangos hints at how methods of collecting and reporting data may influence the results. Opening space for children to share and grapple with observations like these is important in building understandings of the power of data to answer questions, as well as its limitations and potential sources of error or bias.

Collectively and over time, opportunities to gather, represent, and interpret different kinds of data will help children build a foundation of understanding. These early experiences eventually allow them to make sense of abstract ideas like expectation and variation—that is, anticipating what is likely and grappling with how much things differ and why this might occur. Even young children can begin to reason about these complex ideas. For example, Ms. Recinos takes up Sebastián's comment about Leo's absence as an opportunity to engage the children in making a prediction. While many children might predict that Leo would choose whatever fruit they themselves chose or make a guess based on what they know about Leo, eventually they may see that the existing data can also be used as a way to make predictions.

What Children Know and Need to Know About Data

by Linda M. Platas

What is *data*? At the simplest level, it is information that we collect about the world. In order to make this information useful, humans need to be able to classify, sort, organize, represent, and interpret it.

Concepts Underlying Data

In order to make use of data, children need to be able to

- Identify variation

- Classify information

- Sort information

Understanding the Question or Problem

In order to figure out which data can answer questions or solve problems, children first need to understand the question or problem and its context. It can be difficult to figure out exactly what data needs to be collected. There are several considerations to bear in mind:

- **What is measured—the sample.** Answers to some questions can be wrong because the analyst doesn't consider the entire sample. Consider, for example, the following question: *How many of the children enrolled in the class in Room 1 go to the park on the weekend?* If some children are absent when this question is asked and children collect data on only those who are present, their answer may be inaccurate because the sample does not represent all of the children in the room. Children frequently think about the here and now, so they may need help thinking beyond the present moment in order to think about what should be included in the complete sample. In other words, are they collecting all the data that is necessary to answer the question?

- **What is measured—the variations and options.** What if some of the children go to the park every weekend, some of the children go to the park infrequently, and some of the children never go to the park? Children may have a hard time thinking about the universe of options because they tend to think only about what they themselves do and fail to realize that other children may act differently. Thinking aloud about all of the possible options *before* gathering the information can be useful.

- **The frequency of data collection**. If the question is *How many children use the outside water table?*, counting children only on one day won't provide a very good answer. What if some children use it infrequently? Although counting children using the water table for a month would give us a more accurate answer, thinking about how accurate we can be given the real-life constraints is useful.

- **The timing of data collection.** In the previous example, collecting information on the use of the water table on days that it snows would probably not be as accurate as collecting information on a warm day.

Representing the Data

Once data is collected, it must be put in a format that assists in answering the question or solving the problem. If the question is *How many children like wearing sandals?*, we could count how many children raise their hands when asked "Raise your hand if you like wearing sandals," "Raise your hand if you don't like wearing sandals," and "Raise your hand if you don't care either way about wearing sandals, or don't have sandals," and then write the resulting numbers on the board. We could then talk about which number was greater. Even if some of the resulting numbers are large, children can still engage in representing data through bar charts, tally marks, and pictographs. It is important to provide children

with the opportunity to decide how they would want to show someone what they learned and represent it in a way that makes sense to them.

Interpreting the Findings

Interpretation is directly tied to understanding the question or problem. Interpreting the findings within the context of the question is essential. When ascertaining how many classmates frequent a park and to what extent, it is important for children to understand that the question and answer concern only children in Room 1 (not all of the children at the school, in the city, or in the world). When ascertaining which classmates use the water table, it is important for children to understand that the

question and answer concern only the children in Room 1 who are present and get a turn at the table, only for the days that the data was collected (not over the course of a year), and only in the school's location (not at home, at a park, or in another classroom).

In the future, all of these ideas will be built upon as children further ways to represent their data, probability, and generalizability. What a terrific start they have!

For more about young children's data learning, visit the DREME TE Project's website at https:// prek-math-te.stanford.edu.

Adapted, with permission, from L.M. Platas, "What Children Know and Need to Know About Data," *DREME TE Project* (Stanford, CA: Stanford University, DREME Network, 2018).

Assessing Children's Understanding

The interactions illustrated in this chapter, both within informal settings and intentionally structured activities, provide ongoing opportunities to learn about children's ideas about measurement and data. Ms. Torres and Ms. Recinos sometimes keep running records of interesting things children said or did. These notes are helpful for ongoing teaching and can also be shared with children's families and used as documentation for required record keeping.

Ms. Torres organizes her notes by child. Here's what she added to her notes on Samantha for this day:

Child's Name: Samantha

Date: January 10

* Descriptive language — said magnatile house is "tall"

* Comparing height — said she wanted to make house "taller than Priscilla;" said she was "smaller than Priscilla"

Ms. Recinos, on the other hand, organizes her running records by content area. Here's what she added to her records for "math" on the day the class discussed the photo of dogs:

Content Area:
Math/Measurement
What Do You Notice?
(Dogs)

Date: March 15

* Zayra — talked about dogs not in order

* Alyssa — noticed dogs didn't share common origin

* Daniel — thinking about how height can change with age

* Sebastián — biggest means heaviest

Here's what Ms. Recinos noted for "math" on the day they discussed the results of the favorite fruit survey:

Content Area:
Math/Data
What Do You Notice?
(Fruit Survey)

Date: March 20

* Daniel — counted marks to compare and was able to say that they were the same

* César — able to compare subsets ("if it was only kids, then apples would win")

* Victoria — understands how changing her choice would change representation

Neither Ms. Torres nor Ms. Recinos are exhaustive in their record keeping. They usually only have time to jot down a couple of things, and on some days, they don't have time to write anything. But over time, their notes end up providing a lot of information that help them see how the children's understandings are developing and inform the activities they plan and the questions they ask. Their notes also allow them to see when it might be useful to pull a small group of children aside so that they can do some more detailed note-taking or work with individual children using other kinds of assessment tasks. They know that what a child says and does in one setting may be different from another depending on the task at hand, the tools that are available, who the child is working with, and how the child might be feeling on that particular day. The goal is to be able to gather information about the child's understandings over time. This allows teachers to document growth and also learn about the contexts and situations in which children are more likely to demonstrate what they know.

Conclusion

As early childhood educators know, children's curiosities about the environment around them drive much of how they experience and interact with the world. Children continually notice, observe, and take stock of all that is around them, particularly as it relates to themselves. They already know much about measurement and data, but they may talk about their ideas in ways that are not initially seen as mathematical. This chapter has focused on how you might leverage such noticings to support and build more formal understandings and celebrate children's inventiveness in describing their understandings. Consider the children you interact with in your daily life. What might they notice, and how might you find some opportunities to build on their noticings?

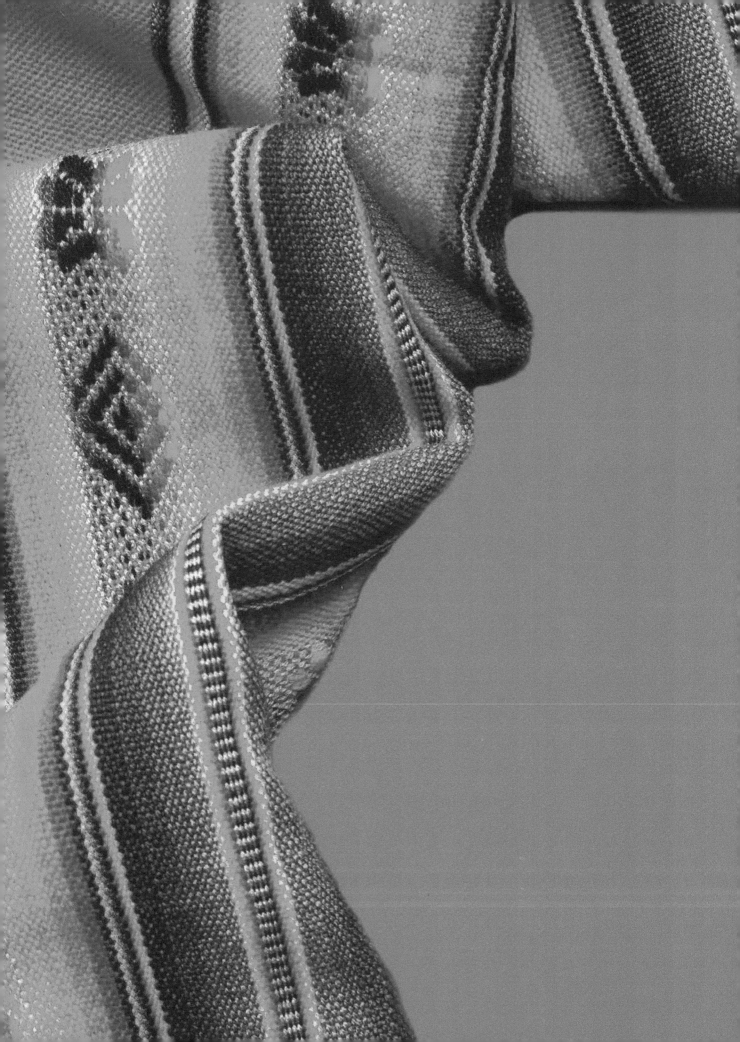

CHAPTER 4
Patterns and Algebra

You might have expected to read about patterns in this book as they are prevalent in early childhood math. Patterning activities are fun to engage children in and can easily be enhanced through creative outlets, such as art and music. Algebra, on the other hand, might feel a little out of place. However, we are not talking about equations with x's and y's, or in other words, the algebra you might remember from your teenage years. Rather, the discussion of algebra explored here is rooted in children's sensemaking of structure and regularities in their environment. This chapter will help you to identify important ideas about patterns and algebra as children engage with things that repeat, are predictable, and they can begin to make generalizations about.

When you hear the word *pattern*, what might first come to mind are simple repeating patterns where two things alternate, often referred to as *ab* patterns: the black and white stripes on a zebra; beads on a string with blue first, then yellow, then blue, then yellow; a stomp, then a clap, then a stomp, then a clap. Children often excitedly notice patterns like these and call out when they see or create them. You also see children recognize and make more complicated patterns where the *pattern unit* (the section of the pattern that repeats) might be a little more involved, like when the bead colors go *blue, yellow, green, red, blue, yellow, green, red*. Identifying patterns is just one part of the important work in this area, and it can provide an entry point into the deeper conceptual work educators hope to engage children in; namely, extending the pattern. One way to think about what this means for teaching is to move beyond wondering "Does the

child call it (*recognize* it as) a pattern?" and "Can the child *name* or *copy* the pattern?"—which is a great first step—and build toward asking "How is the child *extending* the pattern?"

You might have already experienced that children are good at anticipating what will come next; for example, children go through the different parts of your daily classroom routine, usually fairly seamlessly. More importantly, children notice and point out when the routine changes. This happens because children see and understand regularities, and they draw on these understandings to predict what will come next. Working with and thinking about patterns in this way lays the groundwork for developing algebraic reasoning.

Sequences and regularities are everywhere, and children already engage with patterns and algebra through many of their day-to-day activities, with or without a teacher present. The goals of this chapter are to name and address the big ideas of patterns and algebra, highlight how young children already engage with patterns and algebra as they emerge throughout the day, and explore how you might support and extend that engagement. With this in mind, rather than introducing a new Instructional Activity in this chapter, the intertwined nature of children's mathematical thinking and assessment in patterns and algebra is illustrated through three vignettes that take place in spaces likely already familiar to you (and not necessarily during "math time"): a small group of children having a pretend tea party, a child counting as far as he can, and a whole class during story time.

Having a Tea Party in Mr. Patton's Classroom

Calvin and Annie are in the dramatic play area of their preschool classroom, setting up a tea party for themselves and a special guest—Peep, a stuffed bunny. They rummage through a box of plastic dishes on a nearby shelf, looking for just the right ones. Calvin excitedly finds the teacups and puts them on the table. As he starts to spread them out, one for each of the three guests, Annie decides that they also need plates for their pretend snacks. She and Calvin head back to the box to look for plates. They each grab three plates, head back to the table, and start putting out plates next to the teacups. They realize there are enough plates to place two next to each teacup and spread them out. Something about the setup looks a little odd to them as the plates are different sizes. After some trial-and-error rearranging, they happily land on a setup with a teacup, a large plate, and a small plate for each guest.

As soon as the dishes are all arranged, Nuan approaches them to join.

Nuan: I want to play tea party!

Annie: Okay! You can go get your dishes. You need a teacup, a big plate, and a little plate.

Nuan: (*Returns with a teacup and two small plates.*)

Annie: No, you need a big plate.

Nuan: (*Heads back to the box to look for more.*) All the plates are little!

Annie: (*Calls out to the teacher, who is in a nearby area.*) Mr. Patton, Nuan needs a big plate!

Mr. Patton: Okay, go look in the dishes box.

Nuan: We did, but it's only little plates.

> It is the act of extending the pattern that supports Annie in explicitly identifying the pattern unit: "You need a teacup, a big plate, and a little plate." Patterning activities often treat naming the pattern as a foundational first step, but the children show us that attempting to extend patterns can encourage articulating what the pattern is.

Mr. Patton: Sorry, those are all of the dishes that we have. (*Leaves.*)

Annie: But you need a big one.

Nuan: Okay, I'll take this one. (*Takes a large plate from the dishes that are already set up.*)

Annie: No, that one's for Peep. (*Puts the large plate back in its spot.*) It goes teacup, big plate, little plate. The big one is for the snacks.

Nuan: But there's no more big plates.

Annie: Oh . . . (*Shrugs.*)

Calvin: You can have mine. (*Hands his large plate to Nuan.*) I don't like snacks.

Annie: No, but that's yours.

Calvin: It's okay, I don't want snacks. I can have this and this. (*Holds up the teacup and small plate.*)

Annie: No, but then it's not a tea party.

Calvin: Yes, it is . . .

Annie: Then only me and Nuan and Peep are playing tea party and not you.

Calvin: Well, I want to play.

Nuan: I think she wants everyone to have the same everything.

Calvin: Oh, then we can take out all the big plates.

Annie: But then what about the snacks?

Calvin: They can go on the little plates.

Annie: (*Sighs.*) Okaaaay.

Nuan: (*Brings a teapot to the table and begins pouring the tea.*)

Mr. Patton considers for a moment whether he should offer a helpful idea here. However, he chooses not to interfere with the interaction, mainly to give the children the opportunity to negotiate the rules of their dramatic play with each other. He is about to become pleasantly surprised at the important mathematical work that is happening as well!

Calvin's initial peacemaking effort of offering up his large plate to Nuan violates Annie's tea party "rules"—that there is an established pattern unit that must repeat.

The Mathematics of Patterns and Algebra

by Linda M. Platas

Patterns are regularities that we can perceive. We can perceive patterns auditorily (e.g., two fast drum beats followed by one slow drum beat, a bird's call, our heartbeat); visually (e.g., fire truck warning lights, stripes in a sidewalk crossing); somatically, or through tactile or action-based sensations (e.g., tapping one's foot to music, playing those drumbeats mentioned earlier); or as three-dimensional objects (e.g., *one green block, one red block, two blue blocks, one green block, one red block, two blue blocks; daffodil, daisy, daffodil, daisy*). To discern patterns, we must identify the pattern unit. We need to understand not just the individual elements within a pattern unit, but also how the pattern unit is repeated. If you see only *ab*, you don't have enough evidence to identify the pattern. But if you see the *ab* unit repeating, as in *ababab*, then you can be confident of your judgment.

All of these examples are repeating patterns. Our world is also full of different types of *growing patterns. Additive patterns,* which are one kind of growing pattern, add the same amount each time the pattern is extended (e.g., stairs are additive patterns because each step is one unit higher than the previous one). Another kind of growing pattern known as *multiplicative patterns* use scaling (ratios) each time the pattern is extended, such as the pattern of total chairs needed for your classroom tables: one table needs six chairs, two tables need 12 chairs, three tables need 18 chairs, and so on.

Generalization of Patterns

Pattern is considered an early building block in algebra. The ability to generalize patterns contributes to children's later understanding of algebraic equations. For example, adding one more object to a group [N] will always result in N + 1 regardless of whether it is a group of bears, dinosaurs, stairs, or pennies. In the real world, this equation can apply to sets of anything, making the ability to generalize with patterns very useful in understanding the utility (and mathematics) of algebra.

Patterns are sort of like numbers in that the quantity of *two* doesn't specify what there are *two of*, and a pattern doesn't specify what objects, sounds, or actions the pattern is made of. In other words, a pattern described as *abab* can look like *clap, stomp, clap, stomp* or *red bead, blue bead, red bead, blue bead*. Another way of putting it is to say that these different manifestations of patterns (sounds or letters) are *equivalent* to each other. Learning to think about patterns in this way may require a lot of experience working with patterns in many different manifestations.

Pattern Recognition

Pattern recognition begins with the ability to perceive patterns in the world ("Look, my stripes are the same as yours"). Initially, children may not be able to precisely label or describe patterns, but as they gain more language skills, they become able to discern and label them (for example, a child pointing to the series of windows in the classroom and saying, "Teacher, I see it! *Little square, big square, little square, big square*").

Pattern Replication

Replicating a pattern is making a reproduction of a given pattern. As noted above, these patterns can come in many forms, from clapping rhythms to blocks. With exposure to engaging activities, children can learn far more than simple *abab* patterns. Children can also learn to generalize pattern replication by, for instance, creating a *yellow, green, yellow, green* pattern when given the example of a *blue, red, blue, red* pattern (that is, repeating the *abab* in a different color). There is nothing magic about the letters *abab: abab, cdcd,* and *blue, green, blue, green* are all equivalent!

Pattern Extension

Pattern extension activities require identifying and expanding a pattern. Two iterations of the pattern unit (e.g., *abc, abc*) must be provided so that the pattern is evident. Like pattern replication, pattern extension comes in many forms: movements, sounds, objects, and so on.

Pattern Creation

Children can create their own patterns. It is important to help children understand that a pattern unit must repeat in order to be a pattern.

A blue bead followed by a red bead followed by a purple bead is not a pattern; they would need to be followed by another set of these beads in this same order to establish a pattern. The vocabulary relating to this concept isn't as important as helping the children learn that whatever they have chosen as the set of items, sounds, or actions must be repeated in order to create a pattern.

For more about young children's patterns and algebra learning, visit the DREME TE Project's website at https://prek-math-te.stanford.edu.

Adapted, with permission, from L.M. Platas, "The Mathematics of Patterns and Algebra," *DREME TE Project* (Stanford, CA: Stanford University, DREME Network, 2017).

Exploring Children's Thinking: Creating and Extending Patterns

While many early childhood educators will notice the important work the children are doing to communicate and negotiate with each other during this dramatic play interaction, it is important to highlight the powerful engagement around patterns and algebra that is also happening. As Annie and Calvin set up the dishes for the tea party, they decide on a clear pattern unit (a teacup, a large plate, and a small plate) that they want repeated throughout. Not only do the children create a pattern, they begin to engage with a big idea of patterning: what's "allowed" or "not allowed" when extending a pattern. You might also notice that the children's reason for taking on this task is driven by real-life necessity—they want their friend Nuan to be able to join in their play—rather than being imposed on them by the teacher or curriculum.

The group encounters a problem, however, when they realize that they have run out of large plates, and thus they do not have the proper number of pieces to keep the repeating structure consistent and replicate another pattern unit. This isn't just an abstract mathematical dilemma, it's one that has meaningful implications for all of the guests at the party. Excitingly, this situation sparks some problem solving. First, Nuan attempts to take one of the large plates already on the table for her own setup, but that doesn't work as it would break apart Peep's setup (altering an existing pattern unit). Annie, in an effort to explain why this would not work, emphasizes the entire pattern unit again ("It goes teacup, big plate, little plate"), while also highlighting the importance of the large plate in the setup ("The big one is for the snacks"). In response to this, Calvin continues to problem solve as he generously offers up his large plate to Nuan with the rationale that he does not like snacks and therefore does not need a large plate.

Even though Calvin seems happy to play tea party with only one teacup and one small plate, his suggestion does not seem to solve the situation, nor does it satisfy Annie's idea of a tea party. More of Annie's thinking is explained as the children continue to negotiate, and Nuan makes explicit that Annie "wants everyone to have the same everything."

Interpreting this from a mathematical perspective, the pattern unit is important here, and it has to repeat in full for each iteration of the pattern.

Finally, Calvin suggests they can remove *all* of the large plates since there are not enough for the full setup. He alters the original pattern unit from *teacup, large plate, small plate* to just *teacup, small plate* so that they each have the right elements for the pattern to extend. At first, Annie is worried about the snacks and the importance of the large plates, but she does finally agree with Calvin that the small plates can now be used for the snacks. This solution now works: everyone has "the same everything" and the pattern has been extended to all four guests. The children continue on with their tea party play (some, perhaps, a little reluctantly).

Assessing Children's Understanding: Tea Party Patterns

Mr. Patton, who only overheard bits and pieces of the group's negotiation, is curious to explore the pattern ideas that emerged during the tea party. During cleanup time, he takes the opportunity to spend a couple of minutes with this group to find out more about how they were thinking about the tea party setup, specifically how they were thinking about the pattern unit and extending the pattern.

Having a Tea Party in Mr. Patton's Classroom (continued)

Mr. Patton: Your tea party looked fun! Can you tell me a little bit about how you decided to set it up?

Annie: Well, we didn't have enough big plates, so we couldn't do it the way I wanted.

Mr. Patton: Oh, I see. What was the setup that you wanted?

Annie: Like this! (*Rearranges a teacup, a large plate, and a small plate on the table.*) That's what everyone needed, but we didn't have enough.

Mr. Patton: Ahh, that's right. You were asking me for something that you needed.

Annie: We needed a big plate for Nuan. She only had a teacup and a little plate.

Mr. Patton: What did you end up doing?

Calvin: Everyone just had a teacup and a little plate. Because that's all we had. But then everyone could be the same. Teacup, little plate, teacup, little plate . . . (*Points to imaginary spots around the table.*)

Mr. Patton: And what did everyone think of the new setup?

Nuan and Calvin: Good.

Annie: But I didn't get the setup that I wanted. Everyone was supposed to get three.

Mr. Patton: What do you mean everyone was supposed to get three?

Annie: Teacup, big plate, little plate. (*Holds up one finger for each item.*) Three.

Mr. Patton: Oh, but we didn't have the right dishes, so you had to change it so everyone could only . . .

Annie: . . . have two. (*Holds up two fingers.*)

Calvin: Yeah, Annie really wanted teacup, big plate, little plate. Teacup, big plate, little plate.

Annie, Calvin, and Nuan: (*Playfully repeat* teacup, big plate, little plate *and giggle together.*)

Nuan: And if we got the fork drawer too, we could do fork, knife, spoon, fork, knife, spoon.

Annie, Calvin, and Nuan: (*Chant in silly voices while putting away the rest of the dishes.*) Fork, knife, spoon!

Mr. Patton reflects as the children continue to clean up. Even though he missed much of the tea party negotiating, he could tell the group was engaged in some complex mathematical work. He made a conscious decision to stay in the background as much as possible, knowing there was important social and emotional learning as well as mathematical work happening (Platas 2017). After following up with the group and asking them to tell him about the tea party, he is delightfully surprised that the children were not just negotiating a pattern, they were doing so with a situation that was more complicated than a simple alternation of two elements. They were also grappling with understanding the nature of extending and adapting pattern units, or making sense of what repeats (Danielson 2019a).

Mr. Patton is sure to make a quick note of this interaction in his journal so that he can remember to draw upon Annie, Calvin, and Nuan's understanding of pattern and algebra in the future. He wonders if the pattern activities in his curricular materials extend beyond *ab* patterns. If not, he decides that he certainly needs to make sure children have the opportunity to create and engage with more complex patterns.

He also recently learned about Christopher Danielson's (2019b) task of making the smallest version of a pattern as a way to draw attention to the structure of the pattern and the pattern unit; he wonders how he could connect that task to what the children were doing in this situation. Finally, he makes a note about the children applying the patterns to new situations, as they did with the fork, knife, and spoon. He might even use the dishes and cutlery in an upcoming patterning activity.

Counting During an Assessment Task in Ms. Hannah's Classroom

Christopher's teacher, Ms. Hannah, asks him to count out loud as high as he can. He excitedly jumps on this task, saying "One!" even before his teacher finishes asking him. He quickly makes his way through the number sequence past 10 and smoothly through the teens—not a trivial accomplishment for anyone learning counting! As he passes 20, the confidence in his voice is clear as he sharply emphasizes the ones place of each number ("Twenty-*one*, twenty-*two*, twenty-*three* . . ."). When he reaches the end of this decade, he slows down and draws out the last number ("Twenty-niiine") before saying 30, something children regularly do at the end of each decade of numbers.

As Christopher finishes out the 30s, he pauses to ask a question.

Christopher: . . . thirty-seven, thirty-eight, thirty-niiine. . . . Um, what's next? What comes after three? (*Pauses.*) Oh yeah, four! Forty-one, forty-two, forty-three, forty-four, forty-five, forty-six, forty-seven, forty-eight, forty-niiine . . . um, forty . . . um, five-ee . . . um, five-ee-one. Um, what's next again?

Ms. Hannah: (*Pauses, giving Christopher a moment first.*) What did you call it? You said it really nicely.

Christopher: (*Hesitantly.*) Five-ee?

Ms. Hannah: Keep going.

Christopher: Five-ee. . . . (*More confidently.*) Five-ee-*one*, five-ee-*two*, five-ee-*three*, five-ee-*four*, five-ee-*five*, five-ee-*six*, five-ee-*seven*, five-ee-*eight*, five-ee-*nine* . . . sixty! Sixty-*one*, sixty-*two*, sixty-*three* . . .

Christopher continues his counting all the way to an emphatic "One hundred!" with arms raised high. This is followed by a "Can I go outside now?" and a smiling "Yes, of course" from Ms. Hannah.

Exploring Children's Thinking: Patterns in Counting

In school, work on patterns is often separated from other math domains; however, understanding patterns is about understanding structure, and the power of digging deeply into structure is the way that it connects all areas of mathematics. You may not think about numbers when discussing patterning, but they are a mathematically critical space in which to consider patterns and algebra. Putting two amounts together always makes a larger amount. Time is a progression of events; you complete all the parts of your daily routine (e.g., wake up, have breakfast, go to school, eat dinner, have a bath, go to bed) before you start again. In the case of counting out loud, the patterns and structure of our base-10 number system are what allow numbers to keep on going. Did you notice this in Christopher's counting?

In the vignette, Christopher is engaged in a common early childhood assessment task: asking children to count as high as they can to see how much of the counting sequence they know. As you closely observe his excited counting, you start to notice and explore not only that he knows a lot about the counting sequence in general, but that he is specifically drawing on his understanding of patterns and regularities as he continues to count higher.

One place this might stand out is in his counting of the 20s. He clearly emphasizes the ones place of each of those numbers ("Twenty-*one*, twenty-*two*, twenty-*three* . . ."). It is as if you can see him connecting the single-digit sequence (that is, one through nine) that he recited earlier to the current sequence, just with an additional *twenty* in front. As you listen to him count further into other decades (e.g., 30s, 40s), you no longer hear this sharp emphasis, although the regular structure still exists and likely supports him in continuing to count far past the teens. At 29, 39, and 49, Christopher elongates the "niiine" the same way. He does this at the point in the number sequence where a change is going to happen (e.g., from the 20s to the 30s) and he must start to cycle through the numbers again within the next decade. The structure of the base-10 number system and the repeating one through nine support him to go further; all he needs is the name of the next decade number.

When Christopher gets to 39 and 49, he does something interesting and mathematically powerful while he works to remember the next decade. At 39, he questions what the next number should be, knowing that it's definitely not a number that starts with *thirty*. He asks and answers his own question ("What comes after three? Oh yeah, four!"), which supports him in continuing from the 30s into the 40s. In this moment, he is drawing on what he knows about the single-digit sequence and the parallel sequence of decade numbers to help him remember that what comes next is 40. (Do you hear the *four* in *forty*?)

Then Christopher seems to use the same mathematically powerful reasoning to continue past 49. He doesn't ask himself out loud this time, but it is as if he thinks about five coming after four and reasons that the next decade would have to have *five* in its name. (Christopher calls it "five-ee," but it's just as likely that he might have said "five-ty.") He even says a version of 51 ("five-ee-one"), signaling that he knows exactly how to continue into this decade using the structure from earlier in the number sequence. He hesitates here, though, and asks what comes next, not because he doesn't know that two comes after one, but because the names of the numbers don't sound quite right.

What Ms. Hannah chooses to do in this moment is also noteworthy. Whereas many teachers would likely just offer "It's fifty"—understandably so, to help him know that *fifty* comes after *forty*—Ms. Hannah takes a different approach. She encourages Christopher to continue what he started, even though he is hesitant and seems to know that there is something off in what he is saying. With that little bit of reassurance,

Christopher seamlessly continues all the way into the 60s and ultimately all the way to 100! Ms. Hannah knows that Christopher will eventually learn how to say *fifty* through ample continued counting experiences. During this particular experience, she is excited to take the opportunity to support him in trusting his instincts and building on his own knowledge, something she knows will be critical for his lifelong mathematical learning.

Similar to the children in the tea party vignette, Christopher is recognizing and drawing on repeated structure as he counts all the way up to 100. The way he makes use of important pattern and algebra ideas is more complicated here than the tea party, though. The tea party had a simpler pattern structure, one where the children created one pattern unit and repeated it over and over again. The base-10 number system, however, has one repeating pattern that sits within another one, iterating in different yet parallel ways. There is the ones place, with a sequence of single digits (zero through nine) followed by another round of zero through nine, and so on. Every time we get another round of the zero through nine, a new decade number is introduced with a new number name (e.g., *twenty, thirty, forty*) that follows a numeral structure that is parallel to the ones digit (e.g., 20, 30, 40).

While regularity in written numerals (e.g., 1, 2, 3) is consistent throughout the counting sequence, the number names as spoken sometimes mask the underlying structure. This is especially true with the number names *eleven* through *nineteen* in English—*y en español,* once *a* quince (and in Spanish, *eleven* through *fifteen*). These number names do not clearly articulate the numbers' places in the sequence as the number names for 20 and above do. For example, *eleven* and *twelve* do not tell you they are the first and second numbers after *ten*. *Sixteen* sort of sounds like it has the right pieces in the word (*six* and *teen*), just not in the right order; consequently, this often leads to children writing the corresponding numeral as 61 instead of 16 because the *six* is spoken first. There is a pattern, though it takes on a different form. This is why we often hear children mix up or skip numbers between 10 and 20 and why it is important to give children a wide range of experiences in counting beyond 20, even if they are still working on the "tricky teens."

Assessing Children's Understanding: How High Can Christopher Count?

Before Ms. Hannah invites Christopher to count as high as he can, she anticipated that Christopher would count confidently through the teens, as she had seen him do many times, and probably make his way through the 20s. She really does not know what to expect when he reaches 30, though, as she had mainly seen Christopher participate in activities where children counted only to 20. She is so intrigued by how explicitly he uses his knowledge of three and four to count from 30 to 40 and impressed that he counts all the way to 100!

When Christopher reaches 100, Ms. Hannah is of course curious to know if he could count even higher. Alas, she knows that will have to wait for another day as it is more important to recognize his hard work and perseverance by granting his request to go outside than it is to keep counting. After Christopher leaves, she takes a moment to reflect on the other children in her class. She could easily name which children are working on their teens and which ones, like Christopher, seem to know them pretty solidly, at least most of the time. But beyond the teens, how far could the others count? Do they just need a little nudge to be able to build all the way to 100? What if some of them could already count higher in another language? What if some who are still grappling with the teens could actually count through the 20s and 30s accurately?

Seeing how much patterning work Christopher is doing as he counts further and further, Ms. Hannah becomes concerned that she is limiting children's opportunities to go beyond the 20s, even though that is what she thought she was supposed to focus on at this age. With this in mind, she knows exactly what she wants to do and does it right away so she does not forget: she quickly reorganizes some of her counting collections (see Chapter 1) so that she has some larger collections (some with more than 50 objects!) to give children more opportunities to showcase and build their understanding of the number sequence.

Story Time in Teacher Adrian's Classroom

Teacher Adrian receives a copy of the book *Hush! A Thai Lullaby,* by Minfong Ho, illustrated by Holly Meade, as a gift from one of the families at his school. In this lyrical story, a mother is trying to quiet the world so that her baby may sleep. Each turn of the page brings a new animal making its own unique sound that might wake the baby. When the mother hears a sound, she tries to "Hush!" it away with a gentle "Can't you see that Baby's sleeping?" and "My Baby's sleeping right nearby."

Teacher Adrian eagerly reads the book aloud to his class for the first time.

Hush!
Who's that weeping
in the wind?

"Wee-wee, Wee-wee,"
A small mosquito.

Mosquito, mosquito,
don't come weeping.
Can't you see that
Baby's sleeping?
Mosquito, mosquito,
don't you cry,
My baby's sleeping
right nearby.

Hush!
Who's that peeping
from the ceiling?

"TUK-GHAA, TUK-GHAA!"
A long-tailed lizard.

Lizard, lizard,
don't come peeping.
Can't you see that
Baby's sleeping?
Lizard, lizard,
don't you cry,
My baby's sleeping
right nearby.

Hush!

"Wee-wee, Wee-wee,"
A small mosquito.

Mosquito, mosquito,
don't come weeping.
Can't you see that
Baby's sleeping?
Mosquito, mosquito,
don't you cry,
My baby's sleeping
right nearby.

Hush!
Who's that peeping
from the ceiling?

Teacher Adrian begins reading *Hush! A Thai Lullaby* to his class.

From *Hush! A Thai Lullaby*, by Minfong Ho, illustrated by Holly Meade. Text copyright © 1996 by Minfong Ho. Illustrations copyright © 1996 by Holly Meade. Reprinted with permission from the publisher, Orchard Books, an imprint of Scholastic Inc., and McIntosh & Otis Inc.

At first, the children relax on the rug, enjoying the story. However, when Teacher Adrian reaches the third "Hush!" children's voices quietly begin to join him. They say "Hush!" with him and join him in gesturing an index finger to their mouths like the mother in the illustration.

Later in the story, Teacher Adrian no longer does the gesture, nor does he say the "Hush!" at the beginning of each verse. Whenever he reaches another recurring part of the verse (". . . don't you cry, My baby's sleeping right nearby"), he hears a few more voices whispering with him each time, followed by the children smiling and glancing at each other. They chorus "Hush!" as a group, and sometimes giggle in delight as they do so. Quiet voices can also be heard throughout the group as children start to echo other lines in the story, especially the rhyming phrases "don't you cry" and "right nearby."

The story continues with a slow rhythmic flow that emerges from the poetic structure of the words as well as the consistent layout of the writing on each page. Each page turns at the same part of each refrain before revealing the next new animal sound and illustration. When it's time to meet the green frog, however, the text has a different layout than the other pages; it stretches across the page in multiple sections, rather than in one column. Teacher Adrian accidentally skips a line at the bottom left-hand corner of the page because his hand is covering it. Not to worry—the children quickly catch on to this before they get too far ahead.

Teacher Adrian and Children: "Hush!"

Teacher Adrian: "Who's that leaping by the well?" (*Accidentally misses a line.*) "Green frog, green frog, don't come leaping. Can't you see that Baby's sleeping?"

James: Wait! Where's the sound?

Teacher Adrian: We already did the hush together.

James: No, not the hush. The animal sound. You didn't do it.

Benny: Yeah where's the part with the sound? Like *ribbit?*

Elli: Yeah, but it's two times. Like *ribbit, ribbit!*

Teacher Adrian: Oh, you're right! My hand was covering up this part! Let me start at the top again. "Hush! Who's that leaping by the well? Op-op, op-op! A bright green frog."

Children: Op-op! Op-op! (*Giggle.*)

Teacher Adrian: (*Pauses.*) Wait . . . how did you know I skipped a line? This story is brand new.

Benny: The animal has a sound.

Elli: And it's always two times!

Benny: Yeah, it's always like that. All the time.

The text on this two-page spread takes on a different layout.

From *Hush! A Thai Lullaby*, by Minfong Ho, illustrated by Holly Meade. Text copyright © 1996 by Minfong Ho. Illustrations copyright © 1996 by Holly Meade. Reprinted with permission from the publisher, Orchard Books, an imprint of Scholastic Inc., and McIntosh & Otis Inc.

The story continues with the mother hushing many more animals. As they near the end, the structure shifts and the final "Hush!" is followed by a new question: "Is everyone asleep?" As Teacher Adrian reads this, the children sit up a bit straighter, somewhat surprised. They had fallen deeply into the rhythm of the repeating verses, but this new break in the pattern is a signal that the story is nearing completion. Their interest is piqued in finding out how the story will now end. (The mother finally quiets down all of the animals and is now asleep herself . . . next to a smiling, bright-eyed, wide-awake baby.)

Exploring Children's Thinking: Patterns and Algebra in Storybooks

Story time is another a rich space in which to notice, build on, and support children's engagement with patterns and algebraic reasoning. There are many opportunities to engage with mathematical work while reading storybooks to children. (For another example, see Mrs. Jordan and the children exploring spatial relations through a storybook in Chapter 2.) While many math-specific children's books might come to mind (e.g., *Five Little Monkeys Jumping on the Bed,* by Eileen Christelow; *The Doorbell Rang,* by Pat Hutchins; *Feast for 10,* by Cathryn Falwell), it is important to think beyond those "math books." Consider, instead, the storybooks that you simply love to read to children for many different reasons— because they make you and the children laugh together, because the story connects to children's diverse lives in meaningful ways, or even because children ask you to read them again and again.

Children's storybooks often use language patterns that are rhythmic, lyrical, and full of sequences and structures that repeat in a predictable manner. This makes them engaging for the reader and the listener. As young children listen to and absorb these stories, they quickly pick up on these language patterns and what might come next and not only want to listen but join in as well. Consider a book you may be familiar with: *Brown Bear, Brown Bear, What Do You See?* by Bill Martin, Jr., illustrated by Eric Carle.

In this story, there is a simple, predictable structure. On each page, a new colorful animal is inserted into the text—a red bird, a yellow duck, and so on. Children seem to seamlessly join in the telling of this story, even if it's not one they have heard before. How do they do this? They notice the repetition and structure of the text, enhanced by rhyming words at the end of each line. Perhaps a teacher could even engage children further by asking them to generate their own new colorful animal to meet along the way, which would be a lovely way to insert some pattern extension work into this story.

Hush! A Thai Lullaby has a similar but more elaborate structure. It is not surprising that children excitedly join in as Teacher Adrian reads this new story to them; the elegant, predictable writing of the story gives them so many repetitions to pick up on. The "Hush!" that kicks off each verse is perhaps the most noticeable (and most fun!) repetition for children, especially through Teacher Adrian's use of tone and gesture. This is not the only place that children notice regularities, however, as they chime in during other parts of the story.

It is interesting to observe as children follow along the pattern, but perhaps more interesting is when they immediately notice a break in that pattern. This happens when Teacher Adrian accidentally skips a line in reading due to the layout of the text, and James interrupts, "Wait! Where's the sound?" After a little discussion between Teacher Adrian, James, Benny, and Elli, Teacher Adrian remedies his storytelling and goes back to fill in what he missed. It takes a moment, however, for Teacher Adrian to realize that it is quite impressive that the children pick up on this break in the pattern. They aren't yet reading along with him, so how *did* they know he skipped a line when they never heard this story before? Revisiting the contributions of James, Benny, and Elli, you can see that they pick up on the regular structure of the verses and know that after the "Hush!" they should hear a new animal sound (and not just once but twice, as Elli notes). This is exciting from a mathematical perspective as noticing the structure and knowing it should always happen the same way is the beginning of understanding functions and making generalizations—in other words, algebraic reasoning!

Questions from Teachers About Choosing Storybooks
. . . .

I really like the idea of integrating literature with math. Which storybooks would you recommend for engaging children in patterns or other math ideas?

Building on early childhood educators' love for reading with children provides plenty of opportunities to engage in important mathematics work during story time. The example in this chapter emerged from children noticing patterns in the language of the story, and Chapter 2 introduced an Instructional Activity called Describe-Draw-Describe to explore other math content (spatial relations) during storybook reading. There is such a wide range of math opportunities that can arise in almost any storybook, but you can start by focusing on stories that you and children love to read together. Here are some ideas for choosing storybooks and engaging children in the math found there:

- **Look beyond the "math" section of the library.** Don't limit yourself to books that appear to be explicitly mathematical—choose good literature that excites and engages children. Bringing a mathematical lens to *any* book reveals the ways patterns, structure, and other math concepts are embedded in our world, real and imaginary. Of course, you can continue to use your favorite "math" storybooks, but also look beyond them to see the mathematical potential of just about any good book.

- **Choose books that connect to children's lives in a variety of ways.** One powerful reason to engage with literature is so that children see themselves and their lived experiences reflected in the stories. You can leverage this personal connection to also support mathematical connections, using the story to deepen engagement with the math ideas that emerge.

- **Let children's ideas lead the math.** Just like with any other activity, give children space to share their own ideas about what they are seeing, hearing, and noticing. For example, children might be interested in the repeating "black is" word structure in *Black Is a Rainbow Color*, by Angela Joy, illustrated by Ekua Holmes, and come up with their own connections to the color black. Or they might be interested in how the people are seated on the bus in *Last Stop on Market Street*, by Matt de la Peña, illustrated by Christian Robinson, and debate the seating arrangement as each subsequent page shows a different view of the bus interior. When you really dig into it, so much of what captures children's attention is rooted in important mathematics.

Assessing Children's Understanding: Storybook Patterns

In the days after Teacher Adrian's introduction of *Hush! A Thai Lullaby,* he notices that the children love to flip through the book on their own during independent book time. They point to different animals and make animal sounds as they hush each other. When Elli asks Teacher Adrian to read it again, he decides to sit with a small group of children who seem interested. Wanting to pick up on some of the important patterning ideas he saw during story time, he decides to make a little activity out of this interaction. He chooses to read only the first three verses of the book to get children back into the rhythmic flow of this structured story. Then he pauses and says, "Instead of turning the page, why don't we make up the next part of the story together?" He continues to engage with the group, asking questions like "What would the next part start with?," "What animal would you want to come next?," "What sound would that animal make?," and "Who wants to do the next part?"

This chapter shared a couple examples of highlighting patterns and algebra through storybooks, but there are many, many more. Consider the variety of children's books in your own libraries, and you might be pleasantly surprised to discover the multitude of opportunities to work on math through them. Other favorite books of yours might come to mind as excellent resources to support children in engaging in, making explicit, and extending patterns through language as well as through detailed illustrations that reveal patterns in backgrounds, page borders, clothing, and more. There are also books where the patterns grow and build on themselves. Look through your favorite storybook with a mathematical lens. Can you see how patterns and algebra might emerge and be explored? What about other math content?

Conclusion

While *ab* patterns are often the focus of pattern and algebra discussions during the early childhood years, children name, create, interact with, and extend patterns in so many other ways throughout their day. Since patterns are all around us in many different forms, this chapter highlighted the importance of recognizing that engagement with patterns might arise where you least expect it. Building on children's ideas during those moments can be quite powerful. Children regularly show us just how capable they are of sophisticated reasoning and even generalizing. What are some opportunities in informal spaces where you can support children's thinking around patterns and algebra?

A Research Overview of What Young Children Know

Developing an understanding of the breadth and depth of mathematical content and of children's thinking in early mathematics enables teachers to make decisions that benefit children's learning. Young children possess mathematical understandings that are complex and sophisticated (Baroody 2004; Ginsburg 1989; Hughes 1986; Steffe 2004; Van de Rijt, Van Luit, & Pennings 1999). They can count, problem solve, and reason about spatial relations. Children can explain and represent their mathematical ideas from an early age (for reviews of the literature, see Clarke, Cheeseman, & Clarke 2006; Clements & Sarama 2007; Perry & Dockett 2008).

Research documenting young children's mathematical capabilities consistently finds that young children know more than we might expect. This appendix provides an overview of what research says about the development of young children's mathematical ideas within the content areas of counting and operations, spatial relations, measurement and data, and patterns and algebra. Following each research overview is a list of suggested readings written by prominent early childhood mathematics researchers from the Development and Research in Early Math Education (DREME) Network.

Counting and Operations

Children come to school knowing something about how to count. Extensive research has investigated the principled ideas that give counting meaning (Baroody, Lai, & Mix 2006). These principles include

> The stable-order principle (the consistent order of the counting sequence)

> The one-to-one principle (that one number word corresponds to one object)

> The cardinal principle (the last number assigned when counting a collection represents the total number of items in the collection)

Early research suggested that the counting principles were learned in succession: children first learned the counting sequence, then moved to one-to-one correspondence before applying the cardinal principle (Gelman & Gallistel 1978). However, researchers subsequently found that some children demonstrated understanding "out of order;" that is, they could use one-to-one correspondence without yet having perfected the counting sequence (Fuson 1988). These findings raised questions about the robustness of a fixed developmental sequence in counting.

The kinds of understanding that children demonstrated were heavily influenced by the assessment tasks themselves, including how the tasks were posed and the size of the collection the children were asked to count (Fuson 1988; Sarnecka & Carey 2008; Wynn 1990). For example, in assessing 476 3- and 4-year-olds, Johnson and colleagues (2019) found that asking preschoolers to count a large collection of 31 pennies allowed them to show knowledge of counting that was not evident in other tasks, such as counting eight bears arranged in a row or counting out loud as high as they could.

The study also found that children showed a range of understandings of the counting principles. Some could use the cardinal principle or one-to-one correspondence without a completely correct counting sequence, and others demonstrated understanding of the cardinal principle without a full grasp of one-to-one correspondence. These findings add to earlier research and show the benefit of asking children to count larger collections to see

what children know about counting and to recognize that the counting principles will emerge in different orders for children.

Children build on their understanding of counting to solve problems. Researchers find that children as young as age 3 and 4 can solve addition and subtraction problems when provided with concrete materials (Clements & Sarama 2007; Hughes 1986; Huttenlocher, Jordan, & Levine 1994). Carpenter and colleagues (1993) found that 88 percent of kindergartners could provide a correct strategy for solving common addition problems by using concrete materials to model the action in the problem. Turner and Celedón-Pattichis (2011) reported similar findings in bilingual kindergarten classrooms.

Children come to school with the ability to model the action in story contexts and word problems (Carpenter, Hiebert, & Moser 1981, 1983). For example, when presented with a story about having seven cookies and then eating three, children naturally count out seven blocks, remove three, and count the remaining blocks to figure out how many are left. Modeling the action in a story context supports children in solving a range of addition, subtraction, multiplication, and division problems, while solving problems that are not as readily modeled leads to difficulty (Carpenter 1985; Kouba 1989; Riley & Greeno 1988).

Often multiplication problems are expected to be more challenging for children than addition and subtraction problems. However, consider how children can model the following problem: *Juanita has 3 packages of gum, and there are 6 pieces of gum in each package. How many pieces of gum does Juanita have?*

Making three packages and putting six objects in each package follows directly from the story told, and many young children can solve such problems. However, a problem that asks children to compare the number of boys and girls and decide how many more girls there are than boys (subtraction) is not as easy to model; nothing in the story tells children to match up concrete materials (such as counters) representing the girls and boys to figure out the difference. Problem difficulty for children is more related to *how* they solve the problem than the operation itself.

Research on the development of children's mathematical thinking in relation to operations is quite robust, indicating that children's intuitive strategies elegantly build on one another as they become more mathematically sophisticated (Empson, Levi, & Carpenter 2011; NRC 2001). As children model the relationships in problems, over time they come to see that they do not necessarily need to represent every item in the problem. However, even these more abstract strategies still reflect the actions embedded in the problem structure; for example, in the cookie story, the child begins by saying "Seven," then counts back until she has raised three fingers: "Six, five, four." These early strategies provide the base understanding for future strategies and can be leveraged to support learning (Carpenter, Fennema, & Franke 1996).

To be clear, while research maps a trajectory of strategies that children are likely to use in ways that are helpful for teachers, this is not a prescription for what children should or will do when they solve a given problem (NAEYC 2020). In earlier studies of the development of children's strategies and in practice, we see variability in the strategies children choose to use, sometimes because of the type of problem or specific numbers involved and other times because they have more than one strategy they can use and choose the one that serves them well in that context (Carpenter & Moser 1984; Siegler 1994; Steffe et al. 1983).

In addition, young children's ability to make use of their informal knowledge to represent quantities and model a problem's structure is dependent upon how they might (or might not) personally relate to the story's context. Thus, the actual validity of problem-solving assessments is often contingent on a particular child's interest in or understanding of the story context, not just their understanding of the mathematics. Children's ability to successfully navigate the assessment setting also requires that they only selectively draw on their everyday and out-of-school funds of knowledge, while at other times children are required to suspend these resources entirely in favor of what school wants them to do. For example, children quickly pick up that the "school way" to solve problems is to use number facts and symbols ("I know it's supposed to be seven minus three, so can I remember that the answer is four?") and often abandon their more authentic, invented strategies to solve problems the way they think others want them to (e.g., Kazemi 2002).

Suggested Readings from the DREME TE Project

> "The Mathematics of Counting," by Linda M. Platas: http://prek-math-te.stanford.edu/counting/mathematics-counting-0

> "The Mathematics of Operations," by Linda M. Platas: https://prek-math-te.stanford.edu/operations/mathematics-operations-0

> "What Children Know and Need to Learn About Counting," by Herbert P. Ginsburg: https://prek-math-te.stanford.edu/counting/what-children-know-and-need-learn-about-counting

> "What Children Know and Need to Learn About Operations," by Herbert P. Ginsburg: https://prek-math-te.stanford.edu/operations/what-children-know-and-need-learn-about-operations

> "Supporting Executive Functioning During Counting," by Jane Hutchison and Deborah Phillips: https://prek-math-te.stanford.edu/counting/supporting-executive-functioning-during-counting

> "Supporting Executive Functioning Through Operations," by Jane Hutchison and Deborah Phillips: http://prek-math-te.stanford.edu/operations/supporting-executive-functioning-through-operations

Spatial Relations

Spatial reasoning in young children has gained significant attention in recent years as it has been found to be a predictor not only of future mathematical understanding but also of success in reading and high school graduation (Duncan et al. 2007). However, researchers have much to learn about children's knowledge of spatial relations. Although historically considered an innate ability, a meta-analysis of research validates that spatial reasoning is in fact malleable (Uttal et al. 2013). Spatial instruction has been linked to benefits not only in the spatial domain but also in number skills, such as improved calculation and basic magnitude and counting skills (Cheng & Mix 2014; Thompson et al. 2013; Verdine et al. 2014).

Research in geometric and spatial thinking has identified a progression of children's thinking within these content domains (Clements & Battista 1992; Clements & Sarama 2007; Piaget & Inhelder [1948] 1967; Van Hiele 1986). Similar to counting and problem solving, children come to school with geometric and spatial abilities (Clements & Battista 1992; Clements & Sarama 2007; Clements et al. 1999; NRC 2009). In particular, infants and toddlers have demonstrated the ability to locate objects in space using landmark cues, form spatial categories, and perform better than would be expected by chance on mental transformations, including rotations and translations (Levine et al. 1999; Newcombe & Huttenlocher 2000; Quinn 1994, 2004). Clements and his colleagues (1999) reported that more than 90 percent of children from ages 3 years and 5 months to 4 years and 4 months could correctly identify a circle, and 82 percent could point out a square. Sixty percent of children ages 4 to 6 could point out triangles, and 50 percent could point out rectangles.

Young children are capable of more than simply identifying and sorting shapes; they can reason about distinguishing characteristics at an early age (Clements & Sarama 2007; Clements et al. 1999; Lehrer, Jenkins, & Osana 1998). However, attempting to assess geometric and spatial reasoning is often complicated by measures that rely on children's verbal explanations, tying the development of spatial reasoning with language development (Bowerman 1996; Clements & Sarama 2007; Clements et al. 1999; Lehrer, Jenkins, & Osana 1998). Future research concerning the role of language needs to account for broader ways of communicating about geometric and spatial ideas, such as gesturing, and consider measures that allow children to explain their thinking in ways that make sense to them (de Araujo et al. 2018; Moschkovich 2015; Radford 2009; Shein 2012).

Suggested Readings from the DREME TE Project

> **"The Mathematics of Geometry and Spatial Relations," by Linda M. Platas:** http://prek-math-te.stanford.edu/spatial-relations/mathematics-geometry-and-spatial-relations

> **"What Children Know and Need to Learn About Shape and Space," by Herbert P. Ginsburg and Colleen Oppenzato:** http://prek-math-te.stanford.edu/spatial-relations/what-children-know-and-need-learn-about-shape-and-space

> **"Supporting Executive Functioning Through Geometry and Spatial Relations," by Jane Hutchison and Deborah Phillips:** http://prek-math-te.stanford.edu/spatial-relations/supporting-executive-functioning-through-geometry-and-spatial-relations

Measurement and Data

Young children naturally encounter and discuss quantities and can use these ideas to classify and measure (Seo & Ginsburg 2004; Zacharos & Kassara 2012). They can compare two objects directly and recognize if they are equal or not (Boulton-Lewis, Wilss, & Mutch 1996). They know explicitly that if they have some clay and then are given more clay, they now have more than they did before. When measuring, they often depend on perceptual cues—that is, which object "looks" longer, wider, or bigger. Trying to use a standard measuring tool (like a ruler or a measuring cup) is more challenging, and when measuring, children sometimes attend to the number of units, not the size of the units being used to measure (Ebeling & Gelman 1994; Zacharos 2006). Part of the challenge for young children is that measuring requires consideration of continuous (measurable) quantities, like the distance across the table, not discrete (countable) quantities, like a collection of acorns. Children do not necessarily integrate their counting of objects with measurement of continuous quantities (Clements & Sarama 2007). Initially as children acquire skills in length measurement, they make direct comparisons by placing two objects on top of each other or side by side in order to compare them. In these cases of direct comparison, children begin to see that two objects under comparison are equal in length when their ends correspond (Clements & Stephan 2004).

The Pattern and Structure Awareness Project (Mulligan & Mitchelmore 2006) found that preschool children's understanding of measurement could be supported through work on patterning, particularly when focusing on the structures of the patterns. The researchers asked children to compare patterns and talk about the differences and similarities in what they were seeing. They also provided opportunities for children to learn how to break down unfamiliar patterns into smaller patterns they know, or *unitize* (Mulligan et al. 2013).

Working with data in the early years is based in counting and classification. Children begin data analysis by sorting and quantifying collections of objects and then describing the attributes of their groups. In this process, young children are most focused on the particulars—they want to tell you about each button in their group rather than name the categories they've created for them to belong to (Russell 1991). They will then begin to classify responses (name the categories) and use the objects or a drawing to show how they sorted and named their collection.

Suggested Readings from the DREME TE Project

> **"The Mathematics of Measurement,"** **by Linda M. Platas:** http://prek-math-te.stanford.edu/measurement-data/mathematics-measurement

> **"The Mathematics of Data," by Linda M. Platas:** http://prek-math-te.stanford.edu/measurement-data/mathematics-data

> **"What Children Know and Need to Know About Measurement and Estimation," by Herbert P. Ginsburg and Colleen Oppenzato:** https://prek-math-te.stanford.edu/measurement-data/what-children-know-and-need-know-about-measurement-and-estimation

> **"What Children Know and Need to Know About Data," by Linda M. Platas:** https://prek-math-te.stanford.edu/measurement-data/what-children-know-and-need-know-about-data

> **"Supporting Executive Functioning Through Measurement," by Jane Hutchison and Deborah Phillips:** https://prek-math-te.stanford.edu/measurement-data/supporting-executive-functioning-through-measurement

Patterns and Algebra

Pre-algebraic thinking develops from the ability to see, represent, and identify patterns' structural relationships (Carraher et al. 2006; Fox 2006; Ginsburg et al. 2006; Sarama & Clements 2009). Papic and colleagues (2011) found that preschoolers' ability to recognize the structure of a simple pattern is central to the notion of a unit of repeat and the development of composite units necessary for understanding multiplication. This study also provides empirical evidence that young children can develop sophisticated patterning concepts and strategies prior to commencing kindergarten, and that children as young as 4 years old can engage in pre-algebraic thinking.

Several studies have found that young children apply patterning skills in a wide variety of situations, including simple repetition, part–whole thinking, recognizing spatial and geometric patterns, and subitizing (Bobis 1996; Feeney & Stiles 1996; Young-Loveridge 2002; Young-Loveridge, Peters, & Carr 1998). Overall, the research shows that young children are capable of much more than is expected in preschool and, given opportunities to engage

in mathematical experiences that promote emergent generalization, children are capable of abstracting complex patterns.

Young children can also reason about operations and the equal sign in ways that support their understanding of the number system and later formal algebra (Carraher & Schliemann 2007; Clements & Sarama 2007; English 2004; Kaput 2008). Much of this research has been conducted in elementary school and shows that early in elementary school, students are capable of making generalizations and reasoning about the equal sign (Bastable & Schifter 2008; Carpenter & Levi 2000). This research base also has implications for young children in terms of introducing the equal sign as a relation (not the answer comes next) and focusing on understanding what happens when operating on quantities in specific ways related to the situation and in more general ways when joining or comparing quantities (Blanton et al. 2018; Jacobs et al. 2007).

Suggested Readings from the DREME TE Project

> **"The Mathematics of Patterns and Algebra," by Linda M. Platas:** https://prek-math-te.stanford.edu/patterns-algebra/mathematics-patterns-and-algebra

> **"What Children Know and Need to Learn About Patterns and Algebraic Thinking," by Herbert P. Ginsburg:** http://prek-math-te.stanford.edu/patterns-algebra/what-children-know-and-need-learn-about-patterns-and-algebraic-thinking

> **"Supporting Executive Functioning Through Patterns," by Jane Hutchison and Deborah Phillips:** https://prek-math-te.stanford.edu/patterns-algebra/supporting-executive-functioning-through-patterns

Situating What a Child Knows

Mathematics is a cultural practice, one that emerges in communities as people attempt to solve problems in their daily lives (Bishop 1988; Diversity in Mathematics Education Center for Learning and Teaching 2007; Lerman 1994; Presmeg 2007; Stigler & Hiebert 1999). Children's cultural backgrounds and practices, languages, experiences, knowledge, and sense of themselves shape who they are, what they know, and how they participate (NAEYC 2019). Considering mathematics as a cultural practice and viewing children as agents in the process complicates how we make sense of what children know and understand (Christensen 2004; Cook-Sather 2002; Dockett & Perry 2007).

Given that children are sensemakers who bring with them not just mathematical knowledge but their own personal experiences from in and out of school, assessments may not capture the ways that children share what they know (NAEYC 2020; NAEYC & NCTM 2010). In assessments, particularly large-scale studies, children are put in situations where they are asked to respond to tasks that are quite unnatural—and potentially more unnatural for some than others. There is evidence that children are more likely to utilize their mathematical knowledge when the task is natural and meaningful to them (Wager, Graue, & Harrigan 2015). For instance, children's experiences with counting might involve grabbing a big handful of items from a tub and figuring out how many they have, but in an assessment, the child sits as the items are placed in a line by the assessor. What is intended to serve as a scaffold may implicitly communicate that the child's job is to count, but not to move, the objects. In other situations, children who do not respond quickly enough are scored as "incorrect," when their hesitation may not be at all related to their mathematical knowledge (such as when they are expected to show knowledge of subitizing). Children are often asked to use tools that they have never seen before and then are scored on their inability to use them as not knowing. Children are asked to talk with people they do not know, yet there is evidence that who they are talking to influences what they share (Franke et al. 2020; Parks & Schmeichel 2014).

Children's responses and participation in assessment situations reflect efforts to demonstrate competence in unfamiliar situations—situations that, especially for children of color living in economic insecurity, are further complicated by power differentials between the children and the primarily European American adult researchers and assessors (Parks & Schmeichel 2014). Thus, the task that is posed, how it is posed, how it is made sense of by the child, and how the child is positioned and feeling that day will all impact a child's responses and researchers' claims about what children know and understand.

Using this Book to Support Professional Learning

This book is a professional resource for early childhood educators who hope to deepen their learning of early mathematics in a way that has a direct, meaningful impact on their teaching practice. One of the overarching goals of this book is to spark conversation and support learning and collaboration among you and your colleagues.

This may happen as the book is read cover to cover or as select portions of the book are read and discussed either as self-contained readings or in relation to other parts of the book. The following are some suggestions for different ways you might engage with this resource.

Bringing an Instructional Activity into Your Classroom

Artifacts of children's thinking (e.g., work samples, photos, videos, notes) are powerful for collaboration and learning. The Instructional Activities explored throughout this book can be tried out with the children in your classroom, and hopefully be done again and again! Capturing and sharing artifacts of children's thinking from the Instructional Activities is productive for discussions about your teaching practice in relation to the ideas discussed in the chapters.

Choose one chapter from Chapters 1–3 and read it, focusing particularly on the Instructional Activity it features and the vignette(s) that illustrates it:

> Counting Collections (pages 10–14)

> Describe-Draw-Describe (pages 30–33 and 36–37)

> What Do You Notice? (pages 53–57 and 62–63)

After reading, discuss the Instructional Activity with colleagues. During your conversation, consider the following:

> What features of the Instructional Activity are most interesting to you?

> How might the Instructional Activity support many different ways of participating?

> What might you learn about children's thinking during this Instructional Activity?

Try out the Instructional Activity in your classroom and collect artifacts of children's thinking to share with your colleagues. These could be a few photos or short videos as children count and move objects, a small stack of their written representations, or observational notes written by you or a teaching partner as children describe their ideas.

When you meet with colleagues, possible prompts for your conversation might include

> It was exciting when . . .

> I was surprised by . . .

> I wasn't sure what to do when . . .

> Next time, I might . . .

Making Connections Across Math Content

Mathematical ideas are connected and interrelated in important ways, and children often work on a lot of different math concepts at the same time. Each of the classroom vignettes in the Introduction and Chapters 1–4 is followed by discussion of children's thinking related to the specific math content focus of that chapter. However, you might see opportunities to explore other math ideas within that vignette.

Choose one of the following vignettes to reread, and discuss with your colleagues the opportunities for highlighting and scaffolding other, different math concepts:

> Engaging with craft sticks in Ms. Jackson's classroom (page 1)

> "Counting Collections in Ms. Gaxiola's Classroom;" specifically, Penelope's interactions with Ms. Gaxiola (pages 12–13)

> "Building a House During Work Time in Ms. Torres's Classroom" (pages 48–50)

> "Having a Tea Party in Mr. Patton's Classroom" (pages 72–73 and 76–77)

Exploring Informal Spaces

Each chapter explores a variety of informal spaces that exist across the day where children move, interact, play, and more. Though these spaces are not generally considered "math time," children are constantly engaged in important mathematical work, with or without the presence of a teacher.

Chapters 1 and 2 each end with a section comprised of a variety of examples illustrating math learning opportunities that authentically occur in informal spaces. Read through the examples in one (or both!) of these chapters and discuss with colleagues what you notice happening in these examples.

Here are some suggested prompts for your conversation:

> What similarities and differences do you see across the various spaces?

> How would you describe the children's participation in these spaces? How is their participation the same or different from what you might see in more structured learning spaces?

> Imagine you were present and could briefly interact with the child or children. How might you find out more about their mathematical thinking? How would you build on that thinking?

> What other informal spaces would you add to this list?

Creating Classroom Spaces that Support Participation

Portions of the physical spaces of classrooms are described throughout the book. These descriptions can serve as entry points for conversations about aspects of the physical space and environment that support a range of child participation in mathematics.

You might begin these conversations by

> Reading across Chapters 1–4 and collecting examples of the classroom environment. Use the examples to create a list of physical aspects of the classroom environment you hope to establish (or have already established) to support children's participation.

> Choosing a chapter from Chapters 1–4 and looking for how tools or resources are used to support child participation. What do you think is important about using these tools or resources to support children's learning?

Connecting Classroom Practice to Research

Each chapter contains excerpts from DREME TE Project resources that highlight the mathematics of that domain and connections to young children's learning and development. Some related DREME TE Project video resources are also identified throughout the book. Choose a chapter from Chapters 1–4 and the related DREME TE Project resources to support discussions that connect classroom practice to research.

After reading the text and watching the video(s), meet with your colleagues and discuss. Here are some possible questions for reflection:

> What connections do you see across the classroom examples and the important mathematics of that domain?

> What mathematical ideas do you see as most critical for the children you teach?

> How does what you are reading compare to your own experiences with children in preschool and kindergarten settings?

> Based on the research and classroom vignettes, what do you wonder about your children's mathematical thinking?

Connecting Theory to Practice

The Preface and Introduction of this book discuss critical ideas about young children, mathematics, and pedagogy that lay the foundation of the subsequent chapters. Looking across Chapters 1-4, many of these ideas are explicit while others may remain implicit. Engaging in discussions with colleagues supports making connections between theory (the Preface and Introduction) and practice (Chapters 1-4) clearer and developing the understanding needed to extend the ideas explored in these chapters in your own practice.

Read the Preface and Introduction as well as a chapter of your choice from Chapters 1–4. Reflect on the connections you make across these sections of the book. You might structure your reflection in one of the following ways as you share and discuss with a colleague:

> Choose a brief excerpt from the Preface or Introduction that intrigues you (maybe a line that you highlighted while reading). Why does this excerpt intrigue you? What connections do you see between this excerpt and the chapter you chose to read?

> Choose a portion from one of the vignettes featured in Chapters 1–4 that stood out to you. What is happening in the vignette? What connections do you see to an idea from the Preface or Introduction?

> Find an interaction where the teacher recognized and built from children's cultural or linguistic resources. How are you and your colleagues deliberate about capitalizing on these types of opportunities in your own practice?

Connecting to Policy and Standards Documents

Use this book to connect to policy and standards documents for early childhood, particularly those that are local and relevant for your work.

Some possible ways of doing this include the following:

> Read NAEYC's "Advancing Equity in Early Childhood Education" position statement (2019). In what ways do you see its big ideas reflected in the Introduction? In Chapters 1–4?

> Read NAEYC's "Developmentally Appropriate Practice" position statement (2020). In what ways do you see its big ideas reflected in the Introduction? In Chapters 1–4?

> Reference your state's math learning standards. How can these standards be addressed when engaging children in one of the Instructional Activities from Chapters 1–3?

> Identify a common assessment task that you give to young children. How would that assessment task capture the ideas of children's thinking as described in Chapters 1–4? How might you adapt the task to capture additional details of children's thinking?

References

Baroody, A.J. 2004. "The Developmental Bases for Early Childhood Number and Operations Standards." In *Engaging Young Children in Mathematics: Standards for Early Childhood Mathematics Education,* eds. D.H. Clements & J. Sarama, 173–219. Mahwah, NJ: Lawrence Erlbaum.

Baroody, A.J., M. Lai, & K.S. Mix. 2006. "The Development of Young Children's Early Number and Operation Sense and Its Implications for Early Childhood Education." In Vol 2. of *Handbook of Research on the Education of Young Children,* 2nd ed., eds. B. Spodek & O.N. Saracho, 187–221. Mahwah, NJ: Lawrence Erlbaum.

Bastable, V., & D. Schifter. 2008. "Classroom Stories: Examples of Elementary Students Engaged in Early Algebra." In *Algebra in the Early Grades,* eds. J.J. Kaput, D.W. Carraher, & M.L. Blanton, 165–84. Mahwah, NJ: Lawrence Erlbaum.

Bishop, A.J. 1988. "Mathematics Education in Its Cultural Context." *Educational Studies in Mathematics* 19 (2): 179–91.

Blanton, M., Y. Otálora, B.M. Brizuela, A.M. Gardiner, K.B. Sawrey, A. Gibbins, & Y. Kim. 2018. "Exploring Kindergarten Students' Early Understandings of the Equal Sign." *Mathematical Thinking and Learning* 20 (3): 167–201.

Bobis, J. 1996. "Visualisation and the Development of Number Sense with Kindergarten Children." In *Children's Number Learning: A Research Monograph of the Mathematics Education Research Group of Australia and the Australian Association of Mathematics Teachers,* eds. J.T. Mulligan & M.C. Mitchelmore, 17–33. Adelaide, Australia: Australian Association of Mathematics Teachers.

Boulton-Lewis, G.M., L.A. Wilss, & S.L. Mutch. 1996. "An Analysis of Young Children's Strategies and Use of Devices of Length and Measurement." *Journal of Mathematical Behavior* 15 (3): 329–47.

Bowerman, M. 1996. "The Origins of Children's Spatial Semantic Categories: Cognitive Versus Linguistic Determinants." In *Rethinking Linguistic Relativity,* eds. J.J. Gumperz & S.C. Levinson, 145–76. No. 17 in Studies in the Social and Cultural Foundations of Language series. New York: Cambridge University Press.

Carpenter, T.P. 1985. "Learning to Add and Subtract: An Exercise in Problem Solving." In *Teaching and Learning Mathematical Problem Solving: Multiple Research Perspectives,* ed. E.A. Silver, 17–40. Hillsdale, NJ: Lawrence Erlbaum.

Carpenter, T.P., E. Ansell, M.L. Franke, E. Fennema, & L. Weisbeck. 1993. "Models of Problem Solving: A Study of Kindergarten Children's Problem-Solving Processes." *Journal for Research in Mathematics Education* 24 (5): 428–41.

Carpenter, T.P., E. Fennema, & M.L. Franke. 1996. "Cognitively Guided Instruction: A Knowledge Base for Reform in Primary Mathematics Instruction." *Elementary School Journal* 97 (1): 3–20.

Carpenter, T.P., E. Fennema, M.L. Franke, L. Levi, & S.B. Empson. 2014. *Children's Mathematics: Cognitively Guided Instruction.* 2nd ed. Portsmouth, NH: Heinemann.

Carpenter, T.P., M.L. Franke, N.C. Johnson, A.C. Turrou, & A.A. Wager. 2017. *Young Children's Mathematics: Cognitively Guided Instruction in Early Childhood Education.* Portsmouth, NH: Heinemann.

Carpenter, T.P., J. Hiebert, & J.M. Moser. 1981. "Problem Structure and First-Grade Children's Initial Solution Processes for Simple Addition and Subtraction Problems." *Journal for Research in Mathematics Education* 12 (1): 27–39.

Carpenter, T.P., J. Hiebert, & J.M. Moser. 1983. "The Effect of Instruction on Children's Solutions of Addition and Subtraction Word Problems." *Educational Studies in Mathematics* 14 (1): 55–72.

Carpenter, T.P., & L. Levi. 2000. *Developing Conceptions of Algebraic Reasoning in the Primary Grades*. Research report. Madison, WI: National Center for Improving Student Learning and Achievement in Mathematics and Science.

Carpenter, T.P., & J.M. Moser. 1984. "The Acquisition of Addition and Subtraction Concepts in Grades One Through Three." *Journal for Research in Mathematics Education* 15 (3): 179–202.

Carraher, D.W., & A.D. Schliemann. 2007. "Early Algebra and Algebraic Reasoning." In Vol. 2 of *Second Handbook of Research on Mathematics Teaching and Learning*, 2nd ed., ed. F.K. Lester Jr., 669–705. Charlotte, NC: Information Age.

Carraher, D.W., A.D. Schliemann, B.M. Brizuela, & D. Earnest. 2006. "Arithmetic and Algebra in Early Mathematics Education." *Journal for Research in Mathematics Education* 37 (2): 87–115.

Cheng, Y.-L., & K.S. Mix. 2014. "Spatial Training Improves Children's Mathematics Ability." *Journal of Cognition and Development* 15 (1): 2–11.

Christensen, P.H. 2004. "Children's Participation in Ethnographic Research: Issues of Power and Representation." *Children & Society* 18 (2): 165–76.

Clarke, B., J. Cheeseman, & D. Clarke. 2006. "The Mathematical Knowledge and Understanding Young Children Bring to School." *Mathematics Education Research Journal* 18 (1): 78–102.

Clements, D.H., & M.T. Battista. 1992. "Geometry and Spatial Reasoning." In *Handbook of Research on Mathematics Teaching and Learning: A Project of the National Council of Teachers of Mathematics*, ed. D.A. Grouws, 420–64. New York: Macmillan.

Clements, D.H., & J. Sarama. 2007. "Early Childhood Mathematics Learning." In Vol. 1 of *Second Handbook of Research on Mathematics Teaching and Learning*, 2nd ed., ed. F.K. Lester Jr., 461–555. Charlotte, NC: Information Age.

Clements, D.H., & J. Sarama. 2021. *Learning and Teaching Early Math: The Learning Trajectories Approach*. 3rd ed. New York: Routledge.

Clements, D.H., & M. Stephan. 2004. "Measurement in Pre-K to Grade 2 Mathematics." In *Engaging Young Children in Mathematics: Standards for Early Childhood Mathematics Education,* eds. D.H. Clements & J. Sarama, 299–317. Mahwah, NJ: Lawrence Erlbaum.

Clements, D.H., S. Swaminathan, M.A.Z. Hannibal, & J. Sarama. 1999. "Young Children's Concepts of Shape." *Journal for Research in Mathematics Education* 30 (2): 192–212.

Cook-Sather, A. 2002. "Authorizing Students' Perspectives: Toward Trust, Dialogue, and Change in Education." *Educational Researcher* 31 (4): 3–14.

Copley, J.V. 2000. *The Young Child and Mathematics*. Washington, DC: NAEYC; Reston, VA: National Council of Teachers of Mathematics.

Copley, J.V. 2010. *The Young Child and Mathematics*. 2nd ed. Washington, DC: NAEYC; Reston, VA: National Council of Teachers of Mathematics.

Danielson, C. 2019a. "Talking Patterns with Kids." *Talking Math with Your Kids* (blog), February 15. https://talkingmathwithkids.com/blog/talking-patterns-with-kids.

Danielson, C. 2019b. "What Makes a Pattern?" *Overthinking My Teaching: The Mathematics I Encounter in Classrooms* (blog), March 10. https://christopherdanielson.wordpress.com/2019/03/10/what-makes-a-pattern.

de Araujo, Z., S.A. Roberts, C. Willey, & W. Zahner. 2018. "English Learners in K–12 Mathematics Education: A Review of the Literature." *Review of Educational Research* 88 (6): 879–919.

Diversity in Mathematics Education Center for Learning and Teaching. 2007. "Culture, Race, Power, and Mathematics Education." In Vol. 1 of *Second Handbook of Research on Mathematics Teaching and Learning,* 2nd ed., ed. F.K. Lester Jr., 405–33. Charlotte, NC: Information Age.

Dockett, S., & B. Perry. 2007. "Trusting Children's Accounts in Research." *Journal of Early Childhood Research* 5 (1): 47–63.

Duncan, G.J., C.J. Dowsett, A. Claessens, K. Magnuson, A.C. Huston, P. Klebanov, L.S. Pagani, L. Feinstein, M. Engel, J. Brooks-Gunn, H. Sexton, & K. Duckworth. 2007. "School Readiness and Later Achievement." *Developmental Psychology* 43 (6): 1428–46.

Ebeling, K.S., & S.A. Gelman. 1994. "Children's Use of Context in Interpreting 'Big' and 'Little.'" *Child Development* 65 (4): 1178–92.

Empson, S.B., L. Levi, & T.P. Carpenter. 2011. "The Algebraic Nature of Fractions: Developing Relational Thinking in Elementary School." In *Early Algebraization: A Global Dialogue from Multiple Perspectives,* eds. J. Cai & E. Knuth, 409–28. New York: Springer.

English, L.D. 2004. "Promoting the Development of Young Children's Mathematical and Analogical Reasoning." In *Mathematical and Analogical Reasoning of Young Learners,* ed. L.D. English, 201–13. Mahwah, NJ: Lawrence Erlbaum.

Feeney, S.M., & J. Stiles. 1996. "Spatial Analysis: An Examination of Preschoolers' Perception and Construction of Geometric Patterns." *Developmental Psychology* 32 (5): 933–41.

Fox, J. 2006. "Connecting Algebraic Development to Mathematical Patterning in Early Childhood." In Vol. 3 of *Proceedings of the 30th Conference of the International Group for the Psychology of Mathematics Education (PME 30),* eds. J. Novotna, H. Moraova, M. Kratka, & N. Stehlikova, 89–96. Prague, Czech Republic: International Group for the Psychology of Mathematics Education.

Franke, M.L., E. Kazemi, & A.C. Turrou, eds. 2018. *Choral Counting and Counting Collections: Transforming the PreK–5 Math Classroom.* Portsmouth, NH: Stenhouse Publishers.

Franke, M.L., B. McMillan, N.C. Johnson, & A.C. Turrou. 2020. "Connecting Research on Children's Mathematical Thinking with Assessment: Toward Capturing More of What Children Know and Can Do." In *Advancing Knowledge and Building Capacity for Early Childhood Research,* eds. S. Ryan, M.E. Graue, V.L. Gadsden, & F.J. Levine, 55–73. Washington, DC: American Educational Research Association.

Freudenthal, H. 1973. *Mathematics as an Educational Task.* Dordrecht, Holland: D. Reidel Publishing Company.

Fuson, K.C. 1988. *Children's Counting and Concepts of Number.* New York: Springer.

Gelman, R., & C.R. Gallistel. 1978. *The Child's Understanding of Number.* Cambridge: Harvard University Press.

Ginsburg, H.P. 1989. *Children's Arithmetic: How They Learn It and How You Teach It.* 2nd ed. Austin: PRO-ED.

Ginsburg, H.P., J. Cannon, J. Eisenband, & S. Pappas. 2006. "Mathematical Thinking and Learning." In *The Blackwell Handbook on Early Childhood Development,* eds. K. McCartney & D. Phillips, 208–30. Malden, MA: Blackwell.

Ginsburg, H.P., M. Hyson, & T.A. Woods. 2014. *Preparing Early Childhood Educators to Teach Math: Professional Development that Works.* Baltimore: Brookes.

Hughes, M. 1986. *Children and Number: Difficulties in Learning Mathematics.* Oxford: Blackwell.

Huttenlocher, J., N.C. Jordan, & S.C. Levine. 1994. "A Mental Model for Early Arithmetic." *Journal of Experimental Psychology: General* 123 (3): 284–96.

Jacobs, V.R., M.L. Franke, T.P. Carpenter, L. Levi, & D. Battey. 2007. "Professional Development Focused on Children's Algebraic Reasoning in Elementary School." *Journal for Research in Mathematics Education* 38 (3): 258–88.

Johnson, N.C., A.C. Turrou, B.G. McMillan, M.C. Raygoza, & M.L. Franke. 2019. "'Can You Help Me Count These Pennies?': Surfacing Preschoolers' Understandings of Counting." *Mathematical Thinking and Learning* 21 (4): 237–64.

Kaput, J.J. 2008. "What Is Algebra? What Is Algebraic Reasoning?" In *Algebra in the Early Grades,* eds. J.J. Kaput, D.W. Carraher, & M.L. Blanton, 5–18. Mahwah, NJ: Lawrence Erlbaum.

Kazemi, E. 2002. "Exploring Test Performance in Mathematics: The Questions Children's Answers Raise." *The Journal of Mathematical Behavior* 21 (2): 203–24.

Kouba, V.L. 1989. "Children's Solution Strategies for Equivalent Set Multiplication and Division Word Problems." *Journal for Research in Mathematics Education* 20 (2): 147–58.

Lehrer, R., M. Jenkins, & H. Osana. 1998. "Longitudinal Study of Children's Reasoning About Space and Geometry." In *Designing Learning Environments for Developing Understanding of Geometry and Space,* eds. R. Lehrer & D. Chazan, 137–67. Mahwah, NJ: Lawrence Erlbaum.

Lerman, S., ed. 1994. *Cultural Perspectives on the Mathematics Classroom.* New York: Springer.

Levine, S.C., J. Huttenlocher, A. Taylor, & A. Langrock. 1999. "Early Sex Differences in Spatial Skill." *Developmental Psychology* 35 (4): 940–9.

Moschkovich, J.N. 2012. "Mathematics, the Common Core, and Language: Recommendations for Mathematics Instruction for ELs Aligned with the Common Core." Paper presented at the Understanding Language Conference, in Stanford, CA. http://ell.stanford.edu/publication/mathematics-common-core-and-language.

Moschkovich, J.N. 2015. "Academic Literacy in Mathematics for English Learners." *The Journal of Mathematical Behavior* 40 (December): 43–62.

Mulligan, J., & M.C. Mitchelmore. 2006. "The Pattern and Structure Awareness Project (PASMAP)." In Vol. 1 of *Proceedings of the 30th Conference of the International Group for the Psychology of Mathematics Education (PME 30),* eds. J. Novotna, H. Moraova, M. Kratka, & N. Stehlikova, 308. Prague, Czech Republic: International Group for the Psychology of Mathematics Education.

Mulligan, J.T., M.C. Mitchelmore, L.D. English, & N. Crevensten. 2013. "Reconceptualizing Early Mathematics Learning: The Fundamental Role of Pattern and Structure." In *Reconceptualizing Early Mathematics Learning,* eds. L.D. English & J.T. Mulligan, 47–66. New York: Springer.

NAEYC. 2019. "Advancing Equity in Early Childhood Education." Position statement. Washington, DC: NAEYC. www.naeyc.org/resources/position-statements/equity.

NAEYC. 2020. "Developmentally Appropriate Practice." Position statement. Washington, DC: NAEYC. www.naeyc.org/resources/position-statements/dap/contents.

NAEYC & NCTM (National Council of Teachers of Mathematics). 2010. "Early Childhood Mathematics: Promoting Good Beginnings." Joint position statement. Washington, DC: NAEYC. www.naeyc.org/files/naeyc/file/positions/psmath.pdf.

Newcombe, N.S., & J. Huttenlocher. 2000. *Making Space: The Development of Spatial Representation and Reasoning.* Cambridge: MIT Press.

NGA (National Governors Association Center for Best Practices) & CCSSO (Council of Chief State School Officers). 2010. *Common Core State Standards: Mathematics.* Washington, DC: NGA & CCSSO.

NRC (National Research Council). 2001. *Adding It Up: Helping Children Learn Mathematics.* Washington, DC: National Academies Press.

NRC (National Research Council). 2009. *Mathematics Learning in Early Childhood: Paths Toward Excellence and Equity.* Washington, DC: National Academies Press.

Papic, M.M., J.T. Mulligan, & M.C. Mitchelmore. 2011. "Assessing the Development of Preschoolers' Mathematical Patterning." *Journal for Research in Mathematics Education* 42 (3): 237–69.

Parks, A.N., & M. Schmeichel. 2014. "Children, Mathematics, and Videotape: Using Multimodal Analysis to Bring Bodies into Early Childhood Assessment Interviews." *American Educational Research Journal* 51 (3): 505–37.

Perry, B., & S. Dockett. 2008. "Young Children's Access to Powerful Mathematical Ideas." In *Handbook of International Research in Mathematics Education,* 2nd ed., ed. L.D. English, 81–112. New York: Routledge.

Piaget, J., & B. Inhelder. [1948] 1967. *The Child's Conception of Space.* Trans. F.J. Langdon & J.L. Lunzer. New York: Norton.

Platas, L.M. 2017. "Three for One: Supporting Social, Emotional, and Mathematical Development." *Young Children* 72 (1): 33–7.

Presmeg, N. 2007. "The Role of Culture in Teaching and Learning Mathematics." In Vol. 1 of *Second Handbook of Research on Mathematics Teaching and Learning,* 2nd ed., ed. F.K. Lester Jr., 435–58. Charlotte, NC: Information Age.

Quinn, P.C. 1994. "The Categorization of Above and Below Spatial Relations by Young Infants." *Child Development* 65 (1): 58–69.

Quinn, P.C. 2004. "Spatial Representation by Young Infants: Categorization of Spatial Relations or Sensitivity to a Crossing Primitive?" *Memory and Cognition* 32 (5): 852–61.

Radford, L. 2009. "Why Do Gestures Matter? Sensuous Cognition and the Palpability of Mathematical Meanings." *Educational Studies in Mathematics* 70 (2): 111–26.

Riley, M.S., & J.G. Greeno. 1988. "Developmental Analysis of Understanding Language About Quantities and of Solving Problems." *Cognition and Instruction* 5 (1): 49–101.

Rogoff, B. 2003. *The Cultural Nature of Human Development.* New York: Oxford University Press.

Rogoff, B. 2014. "Learning by Observing and Pitching In to Family and Community Endeavors: An Orientation." *Human Development* 57 (2–3): 69–81.

Russell, S.J. 1991. "Counting Noses and Other Scary Things: Children Construct Their Ideas About Data." In *Proceedings of the Third International Conference on Teaching Statistics,* ed. D. Vere-Jones, 158–64. Voorburg, Netherlands: International Statistical Institute.

Ryan, S., M.E. Graue, V.L Gadsden, & F.J. Levine, eds. 2020. *Advancing Knowledge and Building Capacity for Early Childhood Research.* Washington, DC: American Educational Research Association.

Sarama, J., & D.H. Clements. 2009. *Early Childhood Mathematics Education Research: Learning Trajectories for Young Children.* New York: Routledge.

Sarnecka, B.W., & S. Carey. 2008. "How Counting Represents Number: What Children Must Learn and When They Learn It." *Cognition* 108 (3): 662–74.

Seo, K.-H., & H.P. Ginsburg. 2004. "What Is Developmentally Appropriate in Early Childhood Mathematics Education? Lessons from New Research." In *Engaging Young Children in Mathematics: Standards for Early Childhood Mathematics Education,* eds. D.H. Clements & J. Sarama, 91–104. Mahwah, NJ: Lawrence Erlbaum.

Shein, P.P. 2012. "Seeing with Two Eyes: A Teacher's Use of Gestures in Questioning and Revoicing to Engage English Language Learners in the Repair of Mathematical Errors." *Journal for Research in Mathematics Education* 43 (2): 182–222.

Siegler, R.S. 1994. "Cognitive Variability: A Key to Understanding Cognitive Development." *Current Directions in Psychological Science* 3 (1): 1–5.

Steffe, L.P. 2004. "PSSM from a Constructivist Perspective." In *Engaging Young Children in Mathematics: Standards for Early Childhood Mathematics Education,* eds. D.H. Clements & J. Sarama, 221–52. Mahwah, NJ: Lawrence Erlbaum.

Steffe, L.P., E. Von Glasersfeld, J. Richards, & P. Cobb. 1983. *Children's Counting Types: Philosophy, Theory, and Applications.* New York: Praeger.

Stigler, J.W., & J. Hiebert. 1999. *The Teaching Gap: Best Ideas from the World's Teachers for Improving Education in the Classroom.* New York: Simon & Schuster.

Stipek, D. 2017. "Playful Math Instruction in the Context of Standards and Accountability." *Young Children* 72 (3): 8–13.

Thompson, J.M., H.-C. Nuerk, K. Moeller, & R.C. Kadosh. 2013. "The Link Between Mental Rotation Ability and Basic Numerical Representations." *Acta Psychologica* 144 (2): 324–31.

Turner, E.E., & S. Celedón-Pattichis. 2011. "Mathematical Problem Solving Among Latina/o Kindergartners: An Analysis of Opportunities to Learn." *Journal of Latinos and Education* 10 (2): 146–69.

Uttal, D.H., N.G. Meadow, E. Tipton, L.L. Hand, A.R. Alden, C. Warren, & N.S. Newcombe. 2013. "The Malleability of Spatial Skills: A Meta-Analysis of Training Studies." *Psychological Bulletin* 139 (2): 352–402.

Van de Rijt, B.A.M., J.E.H. Van Luit, & A.H. Pennings. 1999. "The Construction of the Utrecht Early Mathematical Competence Scales." *Educational and Psychological Measurement* 59 (2): 289–309.

Van Hiele, P.M. 1986. *Structure and Insight: A Theory of Mathematics Education.* Orlando: Academic Press.

Verdine, B.N., R.M. Golinkoff, K. Hirsh-Pasek, & N.S. Newcombe. 2014. "Finding the Missing Piece: Blocks, Puzzles, and Shapes Fuel School Readiness." *Trends in Neuroscience and Education* 3 (1): 7–13.

Wager, A.A., M.E. Graue, & K. Harrigan. 2015. "Swimming Upstream in a Torrent of Assessment." In *Mathematics and Transition to School: International Perspectives,* eds. B. Perry, A. MacDonald, & A. Gervasoni, 15–30. New York: Springer.

Wynn, K. 1990. "Children's Understanding of Counting." *Cognition* 36 (2): 155–93.

Young-Loveridge, J. 2002. "Early Childhood Numeracy: Building an Understanding of Part–Whole Relationships." *Australasian Journal of Early Childhood* 27 (4): 36–40.

Young-Loveridge, J., S. Peters, & M. Carr. 1998. "Enhancing the Mathematics of Four-Year-Olds: An Overview of the EMI-4S Study." *Journal of Australian Research in Early Childhood Education* 1: 82–93.

Zacharos, K. 2006. "Prevailing Educational Practices for Area Measurement and Students' Failure in Measuring Areas." *The Journal of Mathematical Behavior* 25 (3): 224–39.

Zacharos, K., & G. Kassara. 2012. "The Development of Practices for Measuring Length in Preschool Education." *Skholê* 17: 97–103.

Index

Page numbers followed by *b*, *f*, and *t* indicate boxes, figures, and tables, respectively.

P

Q

R

S

Acknowledgments

This book would not have been possible without the collaboration of an incredible group of early childhood educators.

Dolores Torres, Natali Gaxiola, Allyson Jordan, and Karen Recinos: Thank you for being our thought partners and for being willing to experiment with and share your practice. We are so grateful for the many ways you have pushed our thinking about what young children can do. We are honored to work with you and grateful for your many contributions to the work shared in this book.

To our colleagues in the Development and Research in Early Math Education (DREME) Network, in particular our colleagues Linda Platas, Herb Ginsburg, and Deborah Stipek, who developed the DREME TE resources: Thank you for your many contributions to this book and for your ongoing work with teacher educators. We continue to benefit from your counsel and expertise.

We also appreciate the guidance of our editor, Rossella Procopio, for her work with us.

Writing a book during this challenging year made it even more evident how much we rely on our families, colleagues, and communities to support and inspire us. We would be remiss if we did not mention the many ways that you made this book possible.

This work was funded in part by a generous grant from the Heising-Simons Foundation to the DREME Network.

About the Authors

Angela Chan Turrou, PhD, is senior researcher and teacher educator at the University of California, Los Angeles (UCLA) Graduate School of Education and Information Studies. Her work lives at the intersection of children's mathematical thinking, classroom practice, and teacher learning. In her work with teachers and teacher educators across preschool and elementary settings, Angela leverages purposeful Instructional Activities driven by children's mathematical thinking to support teacher learning, collaboration, and generative growth. She is continually inspired by teachers who, on a daily basis, create space for children to drive the mathematical work and challenge the broader discourse of who does and does not get to be "good at math." Angela is coauthor of *Young Children's Mathematics: Cognitively Guided Instruction in Early Childhood Education* (Heinemann, 2017) and coeditor of *Choral Counting and Counting Collections: Transforming the PreK–5 Math Classroom* (Stenhouse, 2018). Angela lives in Los Angeles, CA. Find her on Twitter @Angelaturrou.

Nicholas C. Johnson, PhD, is assistant professor in the School of Teacher Education at San Diego State University (SDSU). His work investigates how classrooms shape children's opportunities to participate and learn. A former classroom teacher, instructional coach, and county office coordinator, Nick partners with new and practicing teachers to explore children's mathematical ideas and expand what "counts" as math in school. He is a member of SDSU's Center for Research in Mathematics and Science Education, coauthor of *Young Children's Mathematics: Cognitively Guided Instruction in Early Childhood Education* (Heinemann, 2017), and a contributor (with Natali Gaxiola) to *Choral Counting and Counting Collections: Transforming the PreK–5 Math Classroom* (Stenhouse, 2018). Nick lives in San Diego, CA. Find him on Twitter @CarrythZero.

Megan L. Franke, PhD, is professor of education at UCLA. Dr. Franke's work focuses on understanding and supporting teacher learning for both preservice and in-service teachers. She is particularly interested in how teaching mathematics with attention to students' mathematical thinking (Cognitively Guided Instruction, or CGI) can challenge existing school structures and create opportunities for students who are often marginalized to mathematically thrive. Dr. Franke is a member of the Development and Research in Early Mathematics Education (DREME) Network at Stanford University where she is studying pre-K–2 coherence and designing resources for early childhood teacher educators. She lives in Santa Monica, CA. Find her on Twitter @meganlfranke.

More High-Quality STEM Resources

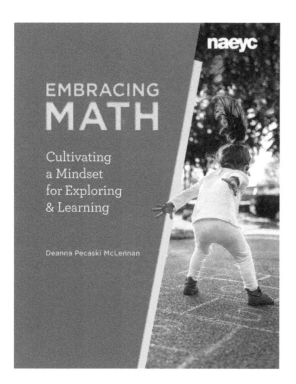

Embracing Math
Cultivating a Mindset for Exploring and Learning

Discover what math teaching and learning look like in the playful, emergent environment of the early childhood classroom. Every day, children explore math concepts in their conversations and interactions. You can build on that natural curiosity by engaging children in meaningful, complex math learning opportunities that are grounded in their observations and questions.

Based on the experiences in her own classroom, author Deanna Pecaski McLennan helps you reflect on your curriculum through a mathematical lens and see the potential for math teaching and learning everywhere. Each chapter of this engaging, easy-to-read book is packed with practical strategies and ideas for fostering hands-on, collaborative, integrated math explorations and inquiries with preschoolers and kindergartners.

2020 • 112 pages
Print: ISBN 978-1-938113-65-9 • Item 1146
☐ E-book: ISBN 978-1-938113-66-6 • Item e1146

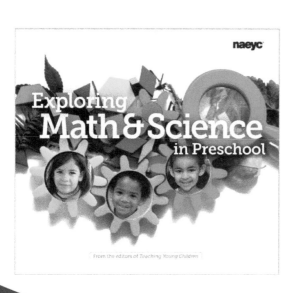

Exploring Math and Science in Preschool

What every preschool teacher needs! Filled with practical strategies and useful information on math and science, this book offers

› Learning center ideas
› Engaging activities
› Practical suggestions that are easy to implement
› Ideas that support the development and learning of every preschooler
› Children's book recommendations

2014 • 112 pages
Print: ISBN 978-1-938113-09-3 • Item 7226

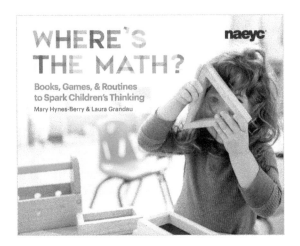

Where's the Math?
Books, Games, and Routines to Spark Children's Thinking

Make math learning both meaningful and fun by building on children's natural curiosity to help them grow into confident problem solvers and investigators of math concepts. Using five math-related questions children wonder about as a framework, this book helps you go deeper into everyday math with children by offering

› A basic overview of math ideas behind matching and sorting, patterns, number sense, measuring, and spatial relationships

› 20 activities appropriate for children in preschool and kindergarten based on new and classic children's books, games, and classroom routines

› Suggestions for individualizing activities for diverse learners

› Examples of intentional questions, comments, and conversations that stretch and focus children's understanding of math concepts

Empower yourself with the guidance and ideas in this practical resource to use play and storytelling to challenge children to think more complexly about the math in everything they see, hear, and do.

2019 • 128 pages
Print: ISBN 978-1-938113-51-2 • Item 1140
E-book: ISBN 978-1-938113-52-9 • Item e1140

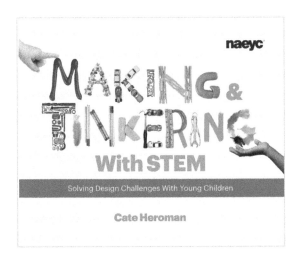

Making and Tinkering With STEM
Solving Design Challenges With Young Children

Teaching and learning STEM subjects (science, technology, engineering, and mathematics) is more accessible than ever before! Children will be inspired, delighted, and challenged as they use everyday materials and STEM concepts to design and build solutions to problems faced by characters in their favorite books. This practical, hands-on resource includes

› 25 engineering design challenges appropriate for children ages 3–8

› Suggestions for creating a makerspace environment

› A list of 100 picture books that encourage STEM-rich exploration and learning

› Questions and ideas for expanding children's understanding of STEM concepts

› A planning template so you can create your own design challenges

2016 • 144 pages
Print: ISBN 978-1-938113-28-4 • Item 1130
E-book: ISBN 978-1-938113-47-5 • Item e1130

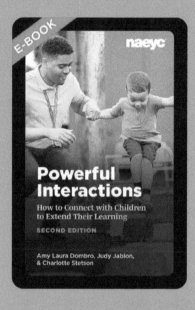

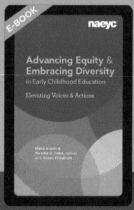

CPSIA information can be obtained
at www.ICGtesting.com
Printed in the USA
JSHW042024270922
31084JS00003B/5